MINNESOTA FARMERS MARKET COOKBOOK

*A Guide to
Selecting and Preparing
the Best Local Produce with
Seasonal Recipes from
Chefs and Farmers*

TRICIA CORNELL
PHOTOGRAPHY BY PAUL MARKERT

Voyageur
Press

For Bruce, Nora, and Arlo, my favorite recipe-testers.

Published in 2014 by Voyageur Press, an imprint of MBI Publishing Company, 400 First Avenue North, Suite 400, Minneapolis, MN 55401 USA

© 2014 Voyageur Press
Text © 2014 Tricia Cornell

Photographs by Paul Markert except where noted.

Voyageur Press titles are also available at discounts in bulk quantity for industrial or sales-promotional use. For details write to Special Sales Manager at MBI Publishing Company, 400 First Avenue North, Suite 400, Minneapolis, MN 55401 USA.

To find out more about our books, visit us online at www.voyageurpress.com.

Library of Congress Cataloging-in-Publication Data

Cornell, Tricia.
Minnesota farmers market cookbook: a guide to selecting and preparing the best local produce: seasonal recipes from chefs & farmers / by Tricia Cornell.
    pages cm
    Includes index.
ISBN 978-0-7603-4486-6 (paperback)
1. Cooking—Minnesota. 2. Cooking, American. 3. Farmers' markets—Minnesota. 4. Farm produce—Minnesota. 5. Local foods—Minnesota. 6. Seasonal cooking—Minnesota. I. Title.
    TX715.C8135 2014
    641.59776--dc23
        2013031246

ISBN-13: 978-0-7603-4486-6

10 9 8 7 6 5 4 3 2 1

Cybervelvet/Shutterstock.com

Front cover photos: Paul Markert
    Top left: Sesame Kale, page 152
    Top center: Grilled Mushroom and Roasted
        Garlic Pizza, page 106
    Top right: Rhubarb-Blueberry Cobbler, page 140

Back cover photos: Paul Markert
    Top: Albaloo Polow, page 61
    Center: Maple Caramel Sauce, page 93
    Bottom: Shaved Asparagus Salad, page 23

Editor: Elizabeth Noll
Design manager: Cindy Samargia Laun
Design and layout: Diana Boger
Cover: Mary Rohl
Maps: Patti Isaacs

CONTENTS

THE FOOD

FOREWORD

I AM OFTEN ASKED what led me to my advocacy for local foods and why I support local and regional farmers who practice sustainable agriculture and raise heirloom crops and heritage breed livestock. I have never been able to give a good answer, since I don't remember ever having looked at food in any other way.

I was brought up in my family's Italian immigrant food culture, which taught me an appreciation for good, healthful food and a love of the land and the farmers who brought it forth. I was cooking dinner for our whole family by the time I was ten. I joined my first food co-op in 1976 at the age of eighteen. As a peripatetic young adult, I would always locate the nearest farm stands, fishmongers, and butchers in whatever town I set up residence. My brother is a horticulturist. Our restaurant, which has a farm-direct market selling local and regional foods attached to it, overlooks the more than 150-year-old Saint Paul Farmers Market. I have been fortunate in many regards when it comes to my relationship with food.

So it is with great joy and a fair modicum of relief that I have observed America's renewed interest in what has come to be called the local food movement. Beginning at the grassroots level, both figuratively and literally, and spurred by enlightened chefs and an ever more sophisticated and demanding public, the local food movement is perhaps best represented by the farmers market.

So what makes farmers markets so special? Aside from the obvious connection to the farmer, which one experiences when shopping at a farmers market, there are many other benefits, including superior taste and freshness, greater nutritional value, and wider variety.

Critics of the local food movement often cite carbon footprint studies showing that more energy is consumed by many small farmers traveling to the market than by the transportation of large quantities of food across great distances. But viewing the benefits of farmers markets through such a narrow lens is rather self-serving. Such a view ignores the aforementioned benefits to consumers as well as the benefits to communities served by the farmers markets. These include the ties

*

Saint Paul Farmers Market, downtown Saint Paul, Minnesota

that are formed between rural and urban populations, the newly found appreciation and understanding forged among various ethnicities, the growth in pride of place that accompanies a connection to a unique food system, and the economic benefit of money remaining in the local economy. I would, of course, be remiss if I didn't mention that a farmers market is also a great gathering place, where neighbors come together to meet and exchange thoughts, ideas, and pleasantries.

I hope the readers of this book take the time to recreate the recipes found herein, and also make plans to visit their local farmers markets more frequently, if they are not already doing so. There are few pleasures in life as wonderful as picking up a fruit or vegetable still warm from the sun and soil, while shaking the hand of the farmer who grew it.

Lenny Russo
Chef and proprietor,
Heartland Restaurant
and Farm Direct Market
Saint Paul, Minnesota
May 13, 2013

ACKNOWLEDGMENTS

I AM PROFOUNDLY grateful to the farmers, chefs, and farmers market staff who so generously shared their recipes and their wisdom, making this book possible. That more than forty hardworking, busy individuals were so giving of their time and expertise is a testament to the strength of the community of people in Minnesota who care about good food. Thank you all.

Heartfelt thanks are also due to Elizabeth Noll from Voyageur Press, who shared her own sharp insight into food, markets, and cooking to shape this project. She also chopped and mixed and measured and shredded and stirred like a tireless pro. And then Paul Markert and Cindy Laun made these dishes look so much better than anything I normally pull off my own stovetop or out of my own oven. And made it fun.

And, of course, my ever patient, ever supportive husband, son, and daughter who tasted so many new recipes and helped wash so very many dishes: Thank you, and I love you.

USING THIS BOOK

IDEALLY, YOU'LL EXPERIENCE this book in the same way you experience your local farmers market. It's organized alphabetically by ingredient, so that you can go straight to what you need, whether that's beets or beef, and quickly find tips for buying, cleaning, storing, and cooking it. Or you can wander through, look for inspiration, and pick up what catches your eye.

In addition to a couple of recipes, each chapter includes simple guidelines for coaxing the best—sometimes unexpected—flavors out of the products you pick up at your market, whether that's a flavor pairing or a cooking method. Many people find cooking more enjoyable when they're exploring suggested techniques; others prefer to follow step-by-step recipes with precisely measured ingredients. This cookbook offers both.

Some of the produce this book explores may be a little unfamiliar—we've included escarole and kohlrabi, for example, because they're found in local farmers markets, and we know some of you have always wondered what to do with them. We also hope you'll also find new ways to look at old favorites such as carrots and broccoli. You can find whole new flavors in fresh produce by trying something raw that you usually cook—or vice versa—or by fixing it with a different group of spices, or by mastering a new cooking technique, such as blanching or pan roasting.

Most of the recipes in this book were contributed by farmers and chefs who have built their reputations on using fresh and local foods. These are folks who know and love Minnesota farmers markets. Because their tastes and cooking styles vary, so do the recipes, from masterfully simple to elaborate and precise. We hope these growers and chefs (and the book itself) become your trusted, friendly companions as you continue to explore Minnesota farmers markets.

A SHORT HISTORY OF MINNESOTA'S FARMERS MARKETS

I'S A LITTLE counterintuitive, but until the past decade, farmers markets in Minnesota were an urban phenomenon.

As long as Minnesota has been a state—longer, even—there has been a farmers market in downtown Saint Paul. In 1853, a two-story building opened at Seventh and Wabasha streets, where locals could buy fruits, vegetables, dairy products, and more brought in by farmers from the surrounding area. The Minneapolis market soon followed in 1876.

Both markets have moved around, as the cities grew and changed around them, and their importance in public and civic life has shifted as well. The downtown Saint Paul market has been in its current home at Fifth and Wall streets since 1982 and the Lyndale Avenue location in Minneapolis has been open since 1937; the freeway simply grew up above it.

In outstate Minnesota, as farmland consolidated and big box stores moved in, farmers markets were rare. A Minnesotan surrounded by neighbors' farms had to know who set up a little farm stand—maybe one with an honor box so no one had to sit there all day—or who wouldn't mind if you knocked on the door to buy an extra half-bushel of tomatoes. There were few central places to buy fresh produce directly from the grower.

As interest in local food began to grow, municipalities and independent non-profits—as well as other entities such as churches, senior centers, hospitals, and restaurants—began to build on the urban farmers market model.

In the early 2000s, there were fewer than 50 farmers markets in Minnesota; in 2009 there were nearly 100. Today there are more than 160. This increase is right on track with the growth in the number of farmers markets around the country, which quadrupled over roughly the same time period. To find more information on the state's farmers markets, contact Minnesota Grown, a program of the Minnesota Department of Agriculture (651-201-6170, www3.mda.state.mn.us/mngrown).

✴
Nicollet Mall Farmers Market, downtown Minneapolis, Minnesota

Minnesota farmers markets are mainly staffed by volunteers and city employees, who add the management of a weekly event and the coordination of vendors to their already full schedules. Some started out as little more than a handful of card tables; some remain that size today. Others attract dozens of vendors and thousands of visitors, who come not just to shop but also to socialize and maybe have a snack and enjoy some entertainment.

As main street shopping districts continue to shrink, weekly or biweekly farmers markets are becoming the new heart of small-town Minnesota. Even in the urban centers, where the large, established farmers markets draw huge crowds, the smaller markets have a critical role: They're giving neighborhoods a new identity and a new reason for neighbors to come together.

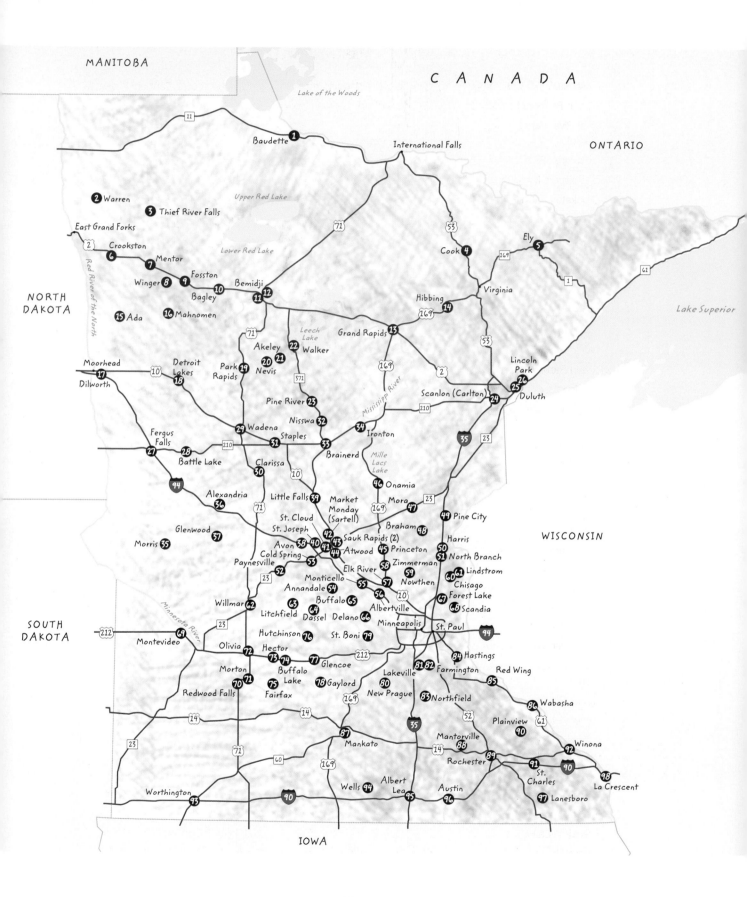

MANITOBA

CANADA

Lake of the Woods

ONTARIO

Baudette **1**

International Falls

2 Warren

Upper Red Lake

3 Thief River Falls

East Grand Forks

Crookston **6**

7 Mentor

Fosston

Winger **8** **9**

Bagley **10**

Bemidji **12**

11

Cook **4**

Ely **5**

Lower Red Lake

Virginia

NORTH DAKOTA

15 Ada

16 Mahnomen

Hibbing

14

Leech Lake

Grand Rapids **13**

Lincoln Park

26

Duluth

25

Lake Superior

Moorhead

17

Dilworth

Detroit Lakes

18

Park Rapids **19**

Akeley **22** Walker

Nevis **20** **21**

Scanlon (Carlton)

24

Pine River **23**

Nisswa **32**

Wadena **29**

34

Fergus Falls

28

27

Battle Lake

Staples **31**

Brainerd **33**

Mille Lacs Lake

Clarissa

30

Onamia **46**

Alexandria

36

Little Falls **39**

Mora

47

Glenwood **37**

St. Cloud

St. Joseph

Braham

48

Pine City **49**

Morris **35**

Avon **38** **40**

42

43

Sauk Rapids (2)

Harris

Market Monday (Sartell)

Cold Spring

41 **44**

Atwood **45** Princeton

50

North Branch

51

Paynesville

53

Zimmerman

58

52

Elk River **57**

59 Nowthen

Lindstrom

60 61

Chisago

Monticello

55

Forest Lake

67

Annandale **54**

Buffalo **65**

56

Scandia

68

Willmar **62**

Litchfield **63**

Dassel

Delano **66**

Albertville

Minneapolis

St. Paul

SOUTH DAKOTA

Montevideo **69**

Olivia

Hutchinson **76**

St. Boni **79**

Hastings **84**

WISCONSIN

Hector

72

73 74

77 Glencoe

Farmington

81 82

Red Wing

Morton

70 71

Buffalo Lake

75

78 Gaylord

Lakeville

80

85

Wabasha **86**

Redwood Falls

Fairfax

New Prague

83 Northfield

Plainview

90

61

Winona **92**

Mankato **87**

Mantorville

88

Rochester **89**

St. Charles

91 **90**

La Crescent **98**

Worthington

93

90

Wells **94**

Albert Lea

95

Austin

96

Lanesboro **97**

IOWA

12

1. Fresh Start Farmers Market
2. Warren Farmers Market
3. Thief River Falls Farmers Market
4. Cook Area Farmers Market
5. Ely Farmers Market
6. Crookston Farmers Market Association
7. Mentor Farmers Market
8. Winger Farmers Market
9. Fosston Farmers Market
10. Bagley Area Farmers Market
11. Bemidji Area Farmers Market
12. Bemidji's Natural Choice Farmers Market
13. Grand Rapids Farmers Market
14. Hibbing Farmers Market
15. Laughing Earth Farmers Market
16. White Earth Community Farmers Market
17. Whistle Stop Park Farmers Market
18. Lakes Area Farmers Market Cooperative
19. Local Farmers Market
20. Nevis Farmers Market
21. Akeley Summer Market
22. The Green Scene/Walker Farmers Market
23. Pine River Market Square
24. Carlton County Farmers Market
25. Duluth Farmers Market
26. Lincoln Park Farmers Market
27. Fergus Falls Area Farmers Market
28. Battle Lake Farmers Market
29. Wadena Farmers Market
30. Hillcrest Farmers Market
31. Staples Area Farmers Market Association

32. Nisswa Farmers Market
33. Brainerd Lakes Area Growers Market
34. Fresh Start Market
35. Morris Area Farmers Market
36. Alexandria Farmers Market
37. Pope County Farmers Market
38. Farmers Market of Avon
39. Little Falls Farmers Market
40. St. Joseph Farmers Market
41. St. Cloud Area Farmers Market
42. Market Monday (Sartell)
43. Central Minnesota Market
43. Sauk Rapids Farmers Market
44. Atwood Memorial Center Farmers Market
45. Princeton Farmers Market
46. Onamia Area Farmers Market
47. Mora Area Farmers Market
48. Braham Farmers Market
49. Farmers Market in the Park
50. Harris Farmers Market
51. North Branch Farmers Market
52. Paynesville Farmers Market
53. Cold Spring Farmers Market
54. Annandale Farmers Market
55. Monticello Farmers Market
56. Albertville Farmers Market
57. Elk River Farmers Market
58. Zimmerman Farmers Market
59. Nowthen Farmers Market
60. Chisago City Farmers Market
61. Lindstrom Farmers Market
62. Becker Market
63. Litchfield Area Farmers Market
64. Dassel Farmers Market
65. Buffalo Farmers Market
66. Delano Farmers Market

67. Forest Lake Farmers Market
68. Scandia Farmers Market
69. Montevideo Farmers Market
70. Redwood Falls Farmers Market
71. Morton Farmers Market
72. Olivia Farmers Market
73. Hector Farmers Market
74. Buffalo Lake Farm & Flea Market
75. Fairfax Farmers Market
76. Hutchinson Farmers Market
77. Glencoe Area Farmers Market
78. Gaylord Farmers Market
79. St Boni Market
80. New Prague Farmers Market
81. Lakeville Farmers Market—Saturday
81. Lakeville Farmers Market—Wednesday
82. Downtown Farmington Farmers Market
83. Northfield Area Farmers Market
84. Hastings Farm Market
85. Red Wing Farmers Market
86. Wabasha Farmers Market
87. Mankato Farmers Market
88. Mantorville Farmers Market
89. Rochester Downtown Farmers Market
90. Plainview Farmers Market
91. St. Charles Farmers Market
92. Winona Farmers Market
93. Worthington Farmers Market
94. Wells Farmers Market
95. Albert Lea Farmers Market
96. Austin Farmers Market
97. Lanesboro Farmers Market
98. La Crescent Farmers Market

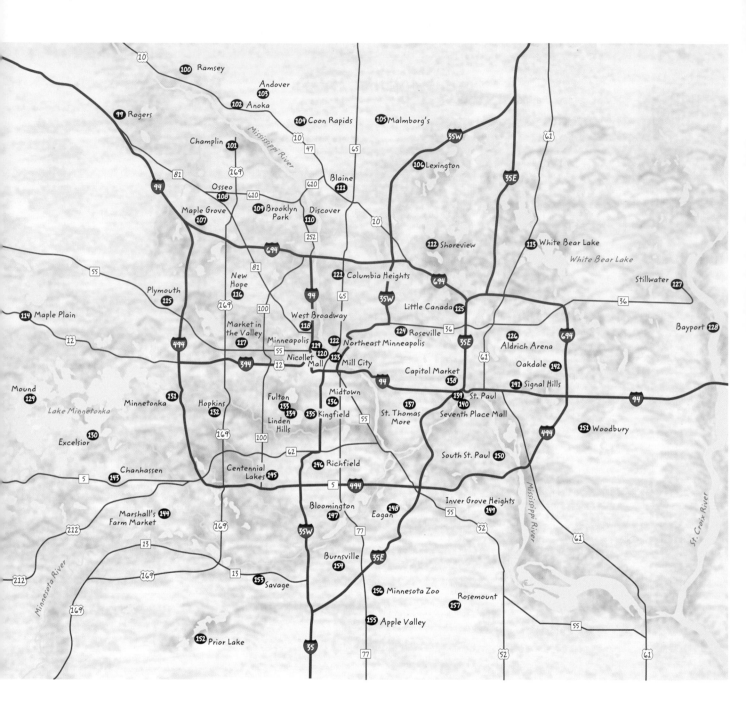

99. Rogers Farmers Market
100. Ramsey Farmers Market
101. Champlin's Farmers Market
102. Anoka Farmers Market
103. Andover Farmers Market
104. Coon Rapids Farmers Market
105. Malmborg's
106. Lexington Farmers Market
107. Maple Grove Farmers Market
108. Osseo Farmers Market
109. Brooklyn Park Farmers Market
110. Discover Farmers Market
111. Blaine Farmers Market: St. Timothy Church
112. Shoreview Farmers Market
113. City of White Bear Lake Farmers Market
114. Maple Plain Farmers Market
115. Plymouth Farmers Market
116. New Hope Community Farmers Market
117. Market in the Valley
118. West Broadway Farmers Market
119. Minneapolis Farmers Market : North Lyndale
120. Minneapolis Farmers Market: Nicollet Mall
121. Columbia Heights Farmers Market
122. Northeast Minneapolis Farmers Market
123. Mill City Farmers Market
124. Roseville Farmers Market
125. Little Canada Farmers Market
126. Aldrich Arena Farmers Market: Maplewood
127. Stillwater Farmers Market
128. Bayport Farmers Market

129. Mound Farmers Market and More
130. Excelsior Farmers Market
131. Minnetonka Farmers Market
132. Hopkins Farmers Market
133. Fulton Farmers Market
134. Linden Hills Farmers Market
135. Kingfield Farmers Market
136. Midtown Farmers Market
137. St. Thomas More Farmers Market
138. Capitol Market
139. St. Paul Downtown Farmers Market
140. Seventh Place Mall Farmers Market
141. Signal Hills Market: West St. Paul
142. Oakdale Farmers Market
143. Chanhassen Farmers Market
144. Marshall's Farm Market
145. Centennial Lakes Farmers Market
146. Richfield Farmers Market
147. Bloomington Farmers Market
148. Eagan Market Fest
149. Inver Grove Heights Farmers Market
150. South St. Paul Farmers Market
151. Woodbury Farmers Market
152. Prior Lake Farmers Market
153. Savage Farmers Market
154. Burnsville Farmers Market
155. Apple Valley Farmers Market
156. Minnesota Zoo
157. Rosemount Farmers Market

APPLES and PEARS

MINNESOTANS ARE FANATICAL about their apples. We scarf them down fresh and baked; when fall comes, we visit orchards by the busload to pick apples and eat cider doughnuts. Many beloved apple varieties, such as the Honeycrisp, were developed in Minnesota. Surprisingly, we are ranked near the bottom of all fifty states in total apple production, but you'd never guess it from the apple displays at local farmers markets.

Apples are great for eating and baking, of course, but they're also a delicious part—or even the star—of many savory dishes. Apples love cheese, onions, pork, cabbage (especially red cabbage), thyme, winter squash, and other flavors that can benefit from a little sweet-tart boost.

Applesauce is a dish that moves especially easily from dinner to dessert, and making your own is as easy as coring and cooking apples until they are soft, then mashing or blending them, depending on whether you like the applesauce smooth or chunky. Add just enough water to keep the apples from sticking to the bottom of the pan. Whether you add sugar or cinnamon during cooking is entirely a matter of taste. You can peel the apples first or cook them with the skins on. The skins will turn the sauce a faint pink but won't add much flavor. You'll need to run the sauce through a food mill or push it through a sieve afterward to remove the peels. Applesauce freezes well and can also be safely canned for later use.

Once you've got applesauce, you're only one step away from apple butter. Cook the applesauce down very, very slowly in a wide pot or slow cooker, stirring occasionally to keep it from sticking, until it is the consistency of soft butter. It will lose at least half its volume. You can add flavors such as cinnamon, ginger, curry, or red wine while it cooks. Apple butter cans and freezes well.

Although we think of apples as the great ambassadors of fall, some varieties are harvested in early August, depending on the weather that year. The earliest apples

WHEN TO FIND IT

Depending on the weather, **apples** are in the market August through mid-October. **Pears** have an even shorter season: mid-August through mid-September.

16

Andrew Brunk/Shutterstock.com

✳
McIntosh apples cook down well into applesauce. Most Minnesota varieties, such as Honeycrisp, SweeTango, and Zestar!, were developed for eating out of hand.

SAVORY STUFFED APPLES

By Molly Herrmann

Molly Herrmann is co-owner and executive chef of Tastebud Catering and Kitchen in the Market, a shared commercial kitchen inside Minneapolis's Midtown Global Market. The kitchen is home to caterers, food trucks, and small commercial manufacturers of everything from soup to pickles, and Herrmann has been a longtime supporter of the local food scene.

If you want to scale down this recipe, to stuff 4 apples instead of 12, for example, it's easiest to make the whole batch of stuffing and reserve the unused portion for later. (It's delicious for breakfast.) Core your apples fairly wide to leave a generous hole for stuffing. Some firmer apples will take longer to soften than others.

1 small butternut squash, peeled, seeded, and diced

Olive oil, about ¼ cup, divided

Salt and pepper to taste

1 medium yellow onion, diced

1 pound Mexican chorizo (raw sausage)

1 cup wild rice, cooked

12 tart apples, cored, leaving 1" bottom on apple

4 ounces shredded cheddar cheese

1 tablespoon smoked paprika

Season butternut squash with olive oil, salt, and pepper. Roast at 400°F until tender.

Cook onion, chorizo, and smoked paprika in a small amount of olive oil until the onion is soft and golden brown and the chorizo is cooked through. Taste and add salt and pepper as needed.

Combine cooked squash with the chorizo mixture and wild rice. Taste again and season as needed.

Fill cored apples with stuffing mixture and place in an oven-proof baking dish. Carefully pour 1" of water into bottom of dish. Cover with foil and bake at 375°F for about 30 minutes, or until apples are just tender.

Uncover, top apples with cheddar cheese and return to oven for 10 minutes or until cheese is melted and apples are tender but not falling apart. Serve on a warm bed of additional stuffing.

Serves 12.

you are likely to see in a Minnesota market are the Beacons, State Fairs, and Zestar!s. Come September, you are likely to see Honeycrisps, Red Barons, and Sweet Sixteens. In late September and early October, the Firesides, Haralsons, Honeygolds, Keepsakes, and Regents appear, with Prairie Spies and Frostbites bringing up the rear. Even the latest bloomers are gone by mid-October.

Generally speaking, the newer Minnesota varieties—Honeycrisp, Zestar!, SweeTango, Frostbite, and SnowSweet—were developed for eating, not for applesauce or pies. For apples that hold their shape well in a pie, look for Regents, Haralsons, and Firesides. For ones that cook down well into applesauce, look for Paula Reds, McIntoshes, and Cortlands.

At the market, look for firm, smooth apples that haven't begun to shrivel and that still feel heavy. If you're making a big batch of applesauce, ask for seconds. These have cosmetic flaws and might have small nicks or bruises but should not have significantly large soft spots or any rot. Be sure to look beyond the top apples in a bushel or box you're considering buying.

Keep apples in a plastic bag in the fridge for up to a month. (Poke a few holes in the bag to let them breathe.)

Crabapples are within the same genus as apples. They are, generally, ferociously

HONEYCRISP APPLE MUSTARD

By Lenny Russo

Make your own mustard? Of course. Lenny Russo has served this mustard at his pioneering Saint Paul restaurant, Heartland, and now you can make it to spread on your corned beef sandwiches or dollop on your pork chop. A quart is a lot of mustard, of course, but once you're making it, you might as well make enough to give away.

1 cup mustard seeds
1 cup mustard powder
2 cups water
3 cups apple cider vinegar
6 tablespoons wildflower honey
6 tablespoons sorghum syrup
2 tablespoons garlic, chopped
6 tablespoons shallots, chopped
1 tablespoon black pepper, freshly ground
½ teaspoon ground allspice
1 teaspoon ground cinnamon
¼ teaspoon ground cloves
1 teaspoon ground mace
1 teaspoon fine sea salt
12 Honeycrisp apples, peeled and cored

Bring the water to boil in a nonreactive saucepot. Add the mustard seeds and mustard powder. Reduce to medium heat and add the remaining ingredients except for the apples. Simmer for 10 minutes.

Meanwhile, dice the apples and roast them in a preheated 350°F oven until they are soft (approximately 15 minutes). Transfer the mustard to a blender and add the apples. Purée until smooth.

Makes about 1 quart.

PEAR SALAD

By Claudine Arndt

Claudine Arndt works with Minnesota Cooks, a project of the Minnesota Farmers Union to promote the wholesome food being produced by our own local growers. She also runs her own health coaching business, Wellness with Claudine, and is a huge fan of farmers markets. "When I go to the farmers market, I can fill my bag for about $20 and get tons of really great food," she says.

When you make this dressing, you can also choose to leave the skin on. It keeps in the fridge for three to five days and can be used on all sorts of salads.

Pear Vinaigrette Dressing	Salad
½ medium ripe pear, peeled, cored, and chopped	10 cups spring mix greens or other greens
3 tablespoons pear, fig, or champagne vinegar	½ large fennel bulb (cored and thinly sliced crosswise)
¼ teaspoon salt	1 ripe pear (such as Comice or Bartlett)
3 tablespoons olive oil	3–4 tablespoons crumbled blue cheese
	3 4 tablespoons chopped walnuts or slivered almonds
	Pear vinaigrette
Purée the pear in a blender with the vinegar and salt. Drizzle in the oil, blending until emulsified.	Combine all ingredients in a large bowl and toss well. Serve immediately.
	Serves four.

tart, as well as dry and woody, so few people enjoy them raw. They are, however, packed with pectin, which is what makes jellies gel, so they are popular in preserves, especially when mixed with other fruits. Make pie filling with them (with far more sugar than in your average apple pie) or poach them in wine for dessert.

Minnesota's pears don't get nearly as much attention as the apples do, but there are varieties of pears that grow well here, including the University of Minnesota's crispy, sweet Summercrisp pear. Your grower may also have Gourmet, Luscious, Parker, Patten, or Ure varieties.

Pears are delicious in crisps and crumbles or peeled and poached whole. They pair well with cheese and nuts, making them perfect for salads and grilled cheese sandwiches. You can cook them down just like apples to make pear sauce and pear butter. They are an unexpected treat on the grill: Slice one in half, scoop out the core, brush it with a little melted butter, and grill it cut side down. Unlike apples, pears are picked before they are ripe. At the market, unless you plan to pick it up and eat it right there, look for pears that are still quite firm. Test the stem end of the pear: If it is soft, the pear is ready for eating. If it is collapsed and shriveling, the pear is headed quickly toward overripe. Pears will ripen in a couple of days on the counter, but if you want to keep them longer than that, put them in the fridge in a plastic bag with a few holes poked in it. Take a pear out of the fridge a day or two before you want to eat it.

ASPARAGUS

ASPARAGUS SPEARS ARE among the first things to peek out of the ground in the spring, and after that they grow so fast that old-time farmers joke they are likely to poke you as you bend over the plant to pick them. That makes them the perfect harbinger of all the great flavors to come as summer arrives. They're gone in a flash, however, so spring is the time to glut yourself with asparagus cooked every way you can imagine.

Fat spears or skinny spears: That's the big debate among asparagus lovers. The truth is that both sides can claim to be right. Fat spears are not necessarily older or any tougher or stringier than skinny spears. (They can be, but it is not a function of their width. Asparagus emerges from the ground at whatever width it's going to be and then grows taller but not wider.)

Fat spears (anything thicker than, say, your pinky finger) are juicy and meaty, but they need to be peeled; otherwise, it can take so long to cook the outer skin that the inside turns to overcooked mush. Skinny spears don't need to be peeled and they cook almost instantly, but they don't have much of that creamy interior that fat spear–enthusiasts love. Skinny spears also have a brighter, greener flavor, thanks to the higher peel ratio.

At the market, buy the ones that look freshest to you and are most uniform in size. (You don't want to be peeling some spears and not others, as they cook differently.) Look for tight, smooth, moist petals at the tip. Tips that have started drying out and opening up are a sign that the asparagus is not fresh. Also, look for a fresh cut at the base of the stalk.

Before cooking, slice off the toughest inch or two at the base. The common advice is to hold each end of a spear between two fingers and bend until it naturally snaps, then discard the end. But sometimes you end up discarding more of the vegetable than you really need to this way. The truly frugal asparagus-lover can also make a nice stock out of the asparagus ends.

WHEN TO FIND IT

There is usually a six-week window, tops, to find local **asparagus**, and that's typically in May and June. Get it while you can.

✴

Fat or thin? Both sizes of asparagus spears can be delicious, if they're fresh.

Unless you have some other use for it in your kitchen, you don't need a fancy asparagus cooker—one of those tall, skinny pots that are meant to hold the asparagus upright so that they steam from the bottom. It's easier to steam asparagus in a regular vegetable steamer, or even lengthwise in a wide pot in about a half inch of water.

To really bring out the best in asparagus, however, you want high, dry heat: roasting and grilling. Toss the spears with just a little oil and salt and put them on the hottest part of the grill or in a very hot oven until they blister. The outside gets crackly while the inside turns almost creamy. After that, a little squeeze of lemon is all you need.

Although we don't often think of it, asparagus can be eaten raw. The skinnier spears are delicious as crudité, and fatter spears can be peeled, then chopped or even shaved, and mixed into salads and dips.

Asparagus will keep for a week or two in a plastic bag in the refrigerator. It is also delicious pickled and can be blanched and frozen as well.

CHILLED ASPARAGUS SOUP with CELERY SEED SOUR CREAM and TOASTED HAZELNUTS

By Lenny Russo

Cold soup, like this one from Russo's Saint Paul restaurant, Heartland, is a wonderful way to welcome the warm June days.

Soup

2 pounds fresh asparagus, trimmed of woody ends

3 spring onions, trimmed

1 cup fresh mint leaves

2 cups court-bouillon (preferably homemade) or low-sodium vegetable broth

1 cup heavy cream (optional)

½ teaspoon fine sea salt

¼ teaspoon white pepper, freshly ground

Sour Cream

1 cup sour cream

1 teaspoon celery seed, lightly toasted

1 pinch fine sea salt

1 pinch black pepper, freshly ground

Garnish

Lightly toasted hazelnuts, papery husks removed and coarsely chopped

Fresh chives, chopped

Plunge the asparagus and spring onions into boiling salted water and cook until tender (approximately 3 minutes). Remove the vegetables from the boiling water and transfer them to an ice-water bath. Let them drain on some paper towels or cloth kitchen towels.

Meanwhile in a nonreactive bowl, whisk together the sour cream and celery seed, and season it with salt and pepper. Set aside in the refrigerator until needed.

When the vegetables have drained sufficiently, coarsely chop them into 1" pieces. Put them in a high-speed blender or food processor. Add the mint and court-bouillon and purée until smooth. Season with the salt and white pepper. With the blender still engaged, slowly add the cream until well incorporated. Chill until needed.

To serve the soup, divide it evenly among six serving bowls. Drizzle or dollop a small amount of the celery seed sour cream over the top. Garnish with hazelnuts and chives.

Serves six.

SHAVED ASPARAGUS SALAD

Fresh asparagus is just as delicious raw as it is cooked and is a surprising base for a salad. If you can only find very skinny asparagus, instead of shaving it, slice the spears into 1" to 2" lengths.

1 pound asparagus, the fattest you can find

Zest and juice of one lemon

2 tablespoons unsalted butter, melted and cooled, but still liquid

¼ teaspoon salt

¼ teaspoon freshly ground pepper

4 hardboiled eggs, quartered

Small bundle of chives, cut into 1" lengths

Trim tough ends off asparagus. Slice off asparagus tops and chop them roughly. Use a vegetable peeler to shave the asparagus into long, thin curls. Whisk together lemon juice, butter, salt, and pepper. Toss all ingredients together and serve immediately.

Serves four.

BEANS, DRIED and FRESH

I T'S TIME TO GIVE beans their due. Sure, they are inexpensive and packed with fiber and protein, but you don't have to be on a budget or a nutrition kick to love beans. When they are good—and cooked well with herbs and aromatics or with cured meats—beans are creamy and flavorful and comforting.

If you're iffy on beans, it may be that you've never had good ones. The farmers market is a good place to find good, fresh beans. Harvesting beans in a small farming operation is labor-intensive, so expect dried beans to be more expensive at the farmers market than at the grocery store. You will, however, likely notice the difference in quality. Fresher beans cook much faster than older beans and have a creamier, more consistent texture.

Look for bags of kidney beans, pinto beans, navy beans, cannellini beans, black beans, cranberry beans, lima beans, split peas, fava beans, and probably some varieties you've never even heard of, very likely sold in one-pound bags (two to three cups of beans). In most recipes you can substitute one kind of bean for another, with the exception of favas, lentils, and split peas, which cook differently from the others.

There are all sorts of opinions on the best way to cook dried beans. The simplest way is in a slow cooker: Cover the beans with about four times as much water and cook on high for about four hours or on low for about eight (check about an hour early, as every slow cooker is different and cooking time will vary based on how fresh the beans are). You can cook them alone for use in other dishes, or you can add aromatics—garlic, onion, fresh or dried herbs, peppers, even a soup bone or bits of your favorite type of cooked meat—right to the pot so that it all cooks together.

If you have a pressure cooker, you can do exactly the same thing—but reduce the cooking time to thirty to forty-five minutes.

Other people soak their beans, covering them in two to three times as much water as beans. This reduces the

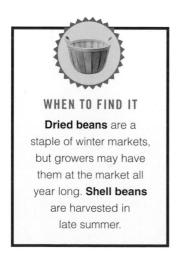

WHEN TO FIND IT
Dried beans are a staple of winter markets, but growers may have them at the market all year long. **Shell beans** are harvested in late summer.

Elena Schweitzer/Shutters ock.com

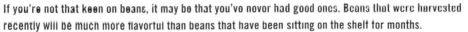

If you're not that keen on beans, it may be that you've never had good ones. Beans that were harvested recently will be much more flavorful than beans that have been sitting on the shelf for months.

cooking time to about an hour or so (again, it varies based on the type of bean and how fresh the beans are). It also allows you to discard the soaking water, which will carry away some of the enzymes that cause gas. Do not soak your beans too long, however. "Overnight" is the general guideline, but it is imprecise. After six to eight hours, the beans may start to ferment, which will give them an off flavor and make them hard on the stomach.

If your dried beans are fresh, you can sometimes cook them quickly: A hard, rolling boil on the stove top for about fifteen minutes and another ninety minutes at a low simmer may do the trick. This wide range of cooking times offers an important lesson: Keep your eye on your beans and test them often to see if they're done. Beans are done before the skin cracks and they turn mushy. Take one out and pinch a bean between your fingers: If it squeezes easily and is uniformly creamy, it's done.

Do not add salt or acids until your beans are finished cooking; that tends to toughen the skins. When they're done, finish them with a pinch of salt and a hit of vinegar and this will help them keep their shape.

The exceptions to everything above, of course, are split peas and lentils, which do not need to soak. They cook in about thirty minutes at a steady simmer (more if you want them to fall apart into a soupy, porridge-like texture). Fava beans must be soaked until you can pry off the tough outer skins with your fingers (about an hour) and then will cook in about 20 minutes at a boil.

Dried beans are easy to store, but they don't keep forever. Any dry container will do, whether in the cupboard or on the counter. Beans that are older than a year are likely too old: You can cook them and cook them and they will never soften up. Ask the farmer when they were dried and mark the date on the package. Dried beans that have started to split, look shriveled, or have especially dull-colored shells are probably too old.

After you have cooked the beans, you can store them in the refrigerator for three to five days or in the freezer for about three months.

Many types of beans are harvested fresh, while the pods are tough but soft and the beans (the seeds, of course) are mature but not dried. These are called "shell beans" or "shelled beans" and will take any bean enthusiast's love to new heights. They are even creamier and more flavorful than their dried counterparts.

✳
1. Cranberry beans. 2. Split peas.

SMOKY SPLIT PEA SOUP

Split pea soup usually gets its smokiness from bacon or some other form of cured pork, but here it comes from whole coffee beans.

¼ cup olive oil

½ red onion, diced

3–4 large garlic cloves, minced

1 teaspoon dried time

1 dried red chili pepper, minced

10 coffee beans

2 bay leaves

½ cup dry vermouth

2 cups yellow split peas

8 cups water

Salt to taste

1 tablespoon good balsamic vinegar

Place first eight ingredients in a heavy-bottomed saucepan and heat slowly over medium-low heat, until onions are very soft, but do not brown, 10–15 minutes.

Add vermouth and turn heat to medium-high and cook until vermouth is nearly boiled off.

Add split peas and water and boil until peas are very soft, about two hours, stirring often to prevent sticking. Blend in batches in a standing blender or with an immersion blender until smooth.

Taste and add salt. Stir in balsamic vinegar.

Serves six.

FRESH SHELL BEAN SALAD

Mild, meaty beans carry the classic flavors of late summer—tomatoes and basil—so well. And a big hit of lemon makes this warm salad bright and satisfying.

3 cups shelled fresh beans

¼ cup olive oil

Zest and juice of one lemon

¼ teaspoon salt

¼ teaspoon freshly ground black pepper

2 large tomatoes, chopped

¼ cup chopped fresh basil

½ cup feta, crumbled

Bring a large pot of salted water to a boil and cook beans until tender, about 20 minutes. Drain and set aside.

Whisk together olive oil, lemon juice and zest, salt and pepper. Toss dressing, beans, and remaining ingredients.

Serves four.

They hold their shape when cooked and are terrific in salads or cooked in a light sauce on the stovetop.

Shelled beans are a finicky crop with a short shelf life, so they aren't all that common in the markets. Cranberry beans and favas are among the ones you're most likely to see. Cranberry beans are particularly beautiful, with pink-and-green shells and white-and-red-swirled beans. (The colors fade when you cook them, sadly.)

At the market, buy more beans than you think you need; it takes a lot of pods to yield a cup or two of beans. Plan to cook them within a day or two and keep them in a loosely covered bowl in the fridge in the meantime. (A plastic bag will promote rot, to which they are especially prone.) The pods should split easily in your fingers, so you can slide the beans into a bowl, and that in itself is a particularly sweet summertime pleasure. Cook the shelled beans in plenty of boiling water for about twenty to twenty-five minutes. (Fresh favas cook much more quickly than when dried—a few minutes in a hot sauté pan should do it—but once you have pried them out of their pods, you'll need to steep them in hot water for a couple of minutes to pop each bean out of its shell.) Drain and let cool for a salad or add them to a skillet of garlic, onions, and greens. Finish with lemon zest or vinegar and you have something close to an ideal summer dinner.

BEEF, BISON, and YAK

F OR CONSUMERS RAISED on fat-marbled beef from corn-fed animals who barely used their muscles, grass-fed beef can take some getting used to. For people such as Abby Andrusko who with her husband, Marcus, runs the Grass Fed Cattle Company, a distributor of grass-fed beef, it can immediately taste just *right* from the first bite.

"Once we tasted grass-fed beef, there was no going back," she says. "The taste was different, at first. It tasted right. It tasted better, full of life, and the way nature should taste."

Grass-fed beef is very lean and shares some similarities with game. Some farmers will cut the difference, raising cattle mostly on grass and then "finishing" them with corn or including corn alongside a mostly pasture diet.

Because it is so lean, grass-fed beef cooks much faster and is easy to overcook, something you want to avoid at all costs.

The easiest way to cook with meat is to divide it into quick-cooking cuts and slow-cooking cuts: fast-cooking steaks (New York strip, sirloin, rib eye, and so on) versus slow-cooking roasts (short ribs, rump roasts, stew meat, and so on).

Abby recommends making steaks less chewy by using a meat tenderizer—that's the spiky square mallet hiding in your utensil drawer—to break down the muscle before cooking the meat, and then let them sit at room temperature for about fifteen minutes instead of plopping them on the grill cold.

There are two schools of thought when it comes to cooking steak. Actually, there are probably thousands when it comes to something as personal and contentious as a delicious steak, but these are the basic lines around which they break down.

Abby Andrusko always uses indirect heat (meaning the cooler part of the grill away from the coals or away from the burner) to cook her steaks.

WHEN TO FIND IT

Some farmers prefer to slaughter their **cattle** in the fall, as feeding them in the winter can be more expensive, but they can be harvested whenever the animal is in the right weight range. You're likely to find meat in the market throughout the market season.

✶

Beef from grass-fed cattle is very lean. Be careful not to overcook it.

Todd Lein, general manager of Thousand Hills Cattle Company, which also raises grass-fed beef, sears his steaks over high heat for about a minute on each side before moving it over to the cooler part of the grill.

Both Andrusko and Lein agree: Take your steak off the grill before it's done. When it is 125 degrees F inside, remove it from the grill, tent it with some foil, and leave it alone for ten minutes. It will simultaneously continue cooking to the recommended 135 to 145 degrees F and reabsorb its own juices. "When you add that much heat," Lein explains, " it causes the muscle to seize up and push out the moisture." If you cut into a steak as soon as you take it off the grill, it will drain delicious juices all over the place and turn out dry and tough.

To make a grass-fed burger, the principle is essentially the same: A nice sear and then indirect or lower heat, but this time until it hits the recommended 160 degrees F (you do have an instant-read thermometer, don't you?). Aficionados may cook their burgers to far lower temperatures (160 degrees F is medium-well), but authorities want you to know you are taking your life in your own hands. (Even if they also cook their own burgers to a nice, rare 130 degrees F.)

When it comes to roasts, the key is low and slow. Andrusko will also pull out the meat tenderizer for a roast, and she will always sear it before cooking it. Lein recommends seasoning the roast overnight—with a little salt and pepper or a little soy

GRASS-FED BRISKET

By Abby and Marcus Andrusko

This is a favorite at the Andrusko house and is known simply as "Marcus's brisket."

Brisket (3 pounds serves four to six people, 5 pounds serves six to eight)
1 bottle of beer
1 bottle of a hot or spicy barbecue sauce
3 sweet onions, quartered
4 cloves of garlic, pressed
1 cup beef stock
Olive oil
Sea salt and ground pepper
1 or 2 cans of pinto beans, drained

Trim any excess fat from meat. Coat with olive oil and rub in sea salt and ground pepper. Let sit in refrigerator overnight.

Heat large skillet or Dutch oven over medium-high heat. Add a thin layer of olive oil and sear brisket on each side for 3–5 minutes. Remove from heat and put on a plate (fat side up) and coat with barbecue sauce.

In a Dutch oven, cook onion and garlic until soft. Add beer, beef stock, and remaining barbecue sauce. Bring to a boil. Remove from heat and add brisket (fat side up). Place lid on and bake in oven at 300°F for 3 hours.

After 3 hours take brisket out of oven and put it on a plate to let it cool. Once it is cool, wrap it in aluminum foil and place it in the refrigerator overnight. Put the Dutch oven in the refrigerator overnight so that the fat separates from the sauce.

The following day, skim the fat off the sauce in the Dutch oven. Cut brisket while cold against the grain in ¼" slices.

Add pinto beans to sauce. Place beef back in sauce and warm for 30 minutes on low to medium on stovetop or in oven.

To make gravy, mix 1–2 tablespoons of cornstarch with a splash of water and desired amount of sauce from Dutch oven. Stir together and warm in saucepan.

BUFFALOAF

Courtesy of Eichten's Hidden Acres

You can make just about anything with bison that you would make with regular beef, as long as you respect how lean the meat is and cook it low and slow.

2 pounds ground bison
1 egg
½ chopped onion
2 teaspoons Worcestershire sauce
Salt and pepper
1½ package crushed soda crackers
½ cup milk
½ chopped green pepper
Garlic salt

Mix all ingredients together and form into a loaf. Bake at 275–300°F for approximately 1 hour.

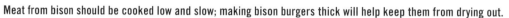

Meat from bison should be cooked low and slow; making bison burgers thick will help keep them from drying out.

sauce—and then searing it and cooking it with broth and vegetables at 325 degrees F for three to four hours. "You just want to run their course," Abby says. "Don't peek."

Bison is also a very lean meat with a distinctive taste—one that's growing in popularity. Tammy Eichten of Eichten's Hidden Acres in Center City, known for local cheeses and bison meat, recommends cooking bison roasts at very low temperatures—as low as 275 degrees F, but for the same length of time you would normally cook a beef roast. Again, use an internal thermometer to keep an eye on the temperature and pull the roast out when it is 10 degrees lower than your desired temperature (135 to 160 degrees F) and let it sit for about twenty minutes before cutting into it.

Ground bison cooks much like ground grass-fed beef. The Eichtens recommend making thicker patties to make juicier burgers, and there's no need to account for shrinkage in the patty, as you might do when forming corn-fed beef burgers.

John and Becky Hooper raise yaks—yes, yaks—at their ranch near St. Cloud and regularly sell their meat at the St. Cloud Farmers Market. They sell yak steaks, ground yak, yak roasts, yak brats, and yak jerky. Their tips for cooking lean yak are familiar: Do not overcook it, cook it low and slow, and use a meat thermometer. Yak is even leaner than grass-fed beef and bison, with as little as 3 percent fat in some cuts.

At the market, look for vendors who are offering samples and, if they haven't got a crowd around the table, are eager to chat about their animals, their farms, and their philosophies.

Fresh meat should be used or frozen within the week. Frozen cuts will keep, in their original vacuum packaging, six months in the regular freezer or a year in the deep freezer.

BISON IN PAPAYA MARINADE with SAUCE CHORON

By Tilia Kitchen

At Tilia, in Southwest Minneapolis, this bison steak is served with braised baby carrots and the braised kohlrabi on page 96. Sauce choron, below, is one of the many variations on béarnaise sauce.

And, yes, the chefs have determined that 24 minutes is the proper marinating time. In fact, they set the timer for 23 minutes and figure on 1 minute to finish whatever else they're doing and get across the kitchen to pull it out. It's important to rinse the marinade off so that it doesn't continue working on the meat. Papaya has enzymes in it that tenderize the meat, but don't make the steak taste particularly fruity.

Bison New York strip steak
(about 4–6 ounces per diner)
1 papaya, peeled and deseeded
6 garlic cloves
1 cup soy sauce
3 cups canola oil

In a blender, puree papaya, garlic, and soy sauce. With the motor running, slowly add canola oil.

Marinate steak in mixture for 24 minutes, then rinse with cold water, and dry with a towel. Grill as you would a grass-fed beef steak.

Sauce Choron

3 egg yolks
2 cups warm
clarified butter
2 teaspoons
minced shallot
¼ teaspoon ground
black pepper
½ cup tarragon vinegar
1 tablespoon cold water
1 teaspoon tomato paste
1½ tablespoons fresh
chopped tarragon
Salt to taste

In a small sauce pot, reduce shallot, black pepper, and vinegar until almost au sec, meaning the pan is almost dry. Cool and reserve.

Using a double boiler and mixing bowl on top, slowly cook the egg, water, and reduction, whisking constantly until egg triples in volume. Be careful to do this slowly so that the egg does not get too hot and curdle. You may have to take it off the heat a few times to ensure proper cooking.

Use a small amount of additional cold water if egg gets too hot or thick.

Once egg is ready, take off of heat and add clarified butter very slowly to allow it to emulsify.

Once butter is fully incorporated, mix in tomato paste and tarragon, and adjust seasoning with salt and additional tarragon vinegar. Adjust consistency with water if needed.

Sauce choron should be held at a temperature of 100°F to 120°F to keep the acid and fat from separating.

✱
Yaks—yes, yaks—are raised in Minnesota. Their meat is extremely lean, with as little as 3 percent fat in some cuts.

YAK AND GREEN CHILE STEW

By John and Becky Hooper

Low and slow is the name of the game when it comes to ultra-lean yak, and a slow cooker is the best tool for that.

2-pound yak roast, cut into ¾" cubes

2 teaspoons dried oregano leaves

1 onion, chopped

1 teaspoon ground cumin

2 or 3 cloves garlic, minced

½ teaspoon ground red pepper

2 14½-ounce cans diced tomatoes with juice

1 7-ounce can diced green chiles

1 8½-ounce can whole-kernel corn, undrained

2 tablespoons yellow cornmeal

Shredded cheddar cheese

Mix all ingredients except the cornmeal and cheese in a 3½-quart slow cooker. Cover and cook on low 7 to 8 hours. Turn to high and stir in cornmeal. Cook on high for 20 minutes. Serve topped with shredded cheddar cheese.

BEETS

BEETS ELICIT PECULIARLY strong opinions in the vegetable world: Some people can't get enough of their sweet, earthy flavor. Others can't get past what they describe as the taste of dirt.

The fact is that beets do taste like dirt: The flavor comes from a compound called geosmin. It's the same thing you smell in the air when the rain falls on dry dirt. So it isn't that beet lovers or beet despisers are tasting different things; it's just a matter of whether you choose to see it as earthy and magical or flat-out dirty.

Beets can be boiled, baked, or roasted, but however you cook them, you should always cook them whole with the peels still on. Otherwise that signature juiciness and flavor will cook right out of them. Leave the roots intact and cut off the stems right at the base. Boiling is a little faster, but some color and nutrients seep out into the cooking water and this method doesn't develop any especially interesting flavors. When it comes to baking and roasting, we need to get our terms straight: Most of us wrap beets in aluminum foil and stick them in the oven. There is nothing wrong with that, but don't call it roasting. Roasting involves a dry heat, and when you trap the steam coming out of the beets inside aluminum foil, you're not roasting.

Truly roasting—as in, placing the beets whole and uncovered on a baking sheet (not straight into the oven, as you do need to catch the juices)—develops deep, caramel flavors and showcases beets' sweetness.

The best way to cook beets, the way that creates the best flavor and texture, is salt roasting. (This does, however, use up a whole lot of salt.) Spread a layer of kosher salt a half-inch thick on a baking sheet or in a roasting dish. Place your beets on top and start pouring salt over them until they are completely covered. You can also stir a tiny bit of water into the salt, until it is the texture of wet sand, to make it adhere more easily to the beets. Bake at 400 degrees F for about 45 minutes.

The salt will pull the moisture out of the beets and hold onto it, forming a hard crust. This creates a little

WHEN TO FIND IT

Overwintered **beets** often appear in the markets first thing in the spring. You can find them again starting midsummer and well into the fall.

mini oven that gets hotter inside. The result is a texture—tender but not the least bit slimy—that you can't get any other way.

Don't trust any beet cooking time in any recipe. Beets are done when you can slip a sharp knife easily through the center. The amount of time this takes varies with the size, age, and type of beet. Count on anywhere from thirty to seventy-five minutes.

The skin will slip right off a boiled beet or one cooked in aluminum foil. Just let it cool until you can bear to touch it and rub it with a paper towel or run it under water. You'll need a knife to coax the skin off a dry-roasted or salt-roasted beet. Don't let them cool too long or they will be hard to peel.

Beets can also, surprisingly, be eaten raw. Finely grated, julienned, or sliced paper thin (a mandoline is great for this), they are a great addition to salads.

Not all beets are deep red. Golden and Chioggia beets have become easier to find at markets. The taste differences are subtle (they are slightly less sweet) and you can use them in any recipe that calls for beets. Chioggia beets are striped pink and white inside, but their bright color fades when you cook them, so consider showing them off in raw slices.

At the market, look for beets with the greens attached. This is for two reasons: Those greens are a good indicator of how fresh the beets are, and the greens are good to eat on their own.

Robert Stone/Shutterstock.com

✳
There are many ways to cook beets, and roasting is one of the best: The dry heat brings out beets' deep, caramel flavors.

ROASTED BEETS WITH LEMON

By David Van Eeckhout

David Van Eeckhout has been farming at Hog's Back Farm, a community-supported agriculture (CSA) farm in western Wisconsin for more than a decade. He and his wife, Melinda, a talented professional chef, take great pride not just in growing delicious vegetables—hundreds of varieties of them—but also in preparing them with care.

"This is a very simple dish and therefore relies on high-quality ingredients," David says. "This is something we'll make in the wintertime when there are plenty of lemons around and we want to splurge on a rich green olive oil from last fall's pressing."

Sometimes he adds roasted pecans, parsley, or dried tomatoes to this salad, and he might also replace the lemon juice and zest with orange or grapefruit.

3 medium beets, about
    1½ pounds
1 tablespoon canola oil
1 clove garlic, sliced as thinly
    as possible
1 tablespoon lemon zest strips,
    1" long by ½ mm wide
3 tablespoons fresh-squeezed
    lemon juice
6 tablespoons extra-virgin olive
    oil, preferably newly pressed
1 teaspoon honey
Sea salt and pepper to taste

Oil the beets with the canola oil and pierce them several times with a fork or knife. Roast on a cookie sheet at 350°F until tender, at least an hour, longer for larger beets.

While the beets are roasting, prepare the garlic and lemon zest. To make them both less pungent, put them in a small strainer and, holding the strainer over the sink, slowly pour boiling water over them two or three times for about 5 seconds each time. Combine the lemon juice, olive oil, and honey, and whisk in the garlic and lemon zest.

When the beets have cooled just enough to handle, peel with a sharp knife. Slice the beets in half and then into ¼" slices. Transfer to a large enough bowl to toss them when dressed.

Add the dressing to the beets and toss to coat liberally. Add salt and pepper to taste.

Vesna Cvorovic/Shutterstock.com

✴
Don't throw away beet leaves. The tops can be chopped and sautéed or used as a spinach substitute.

Beets are relatives of Swiss chard (or the other way around: Swiss chard is a newer variety of beet that has been purposefully bred for its colorful leaves rather than its bulbous root). And the tops, provided they are in good shape, are especially tasty. That proviso is important, because not every grower expects the beet greens to be eaten, so they may be sunburnt or gnawed through by insects or a little beat up by the harvester. If that's the case, the beets themselves are still good, but you'll want to skip the tops.

Wash the beet tops well in plenty of cool water; their crinkly folds are notorious for holding onto dirt. You can chop them and sauté them just like that or toss them into soups, but they'll hold their bright green flavor if you blanch them first. (See page 180 for more about blanching.) Beet tops taste ever so slightly sour and can be used in just about any recipe that calls for spinach.

To store beets, cut off the tops right at the base. The tops will keep about a week if wrapped in a paper towel inside a plastic bag. The beets will keep several months in a plastic bag in the crisper, but you do need to keep an eye on the ends where the tops were: That's where they start to rot.

BEET RISOTTO

By Eric Larsen

Eric Larsen farms smack dab in the middle of the Minneapolis–Saint Paul metro area, on 16 separate plots. He and his partners in Stone's Throw Urban Farm grow more than 30,000 pounds of vegetables, which they sell to CSA members and restaurants, as well as at local farmers markets.

Larsen says he finds selling at the market exciting. "It's fun to talk with people and share ideas," he says. He got interested in cooking just after college and has hosted a Monday night dinner for about two dozen people for the past several years. He created his beet risotto for a Halloween-themed party and has kept it in the rotation ever since.

1 large beet	½ small onion, finely chopped	½ teaspoon salt
1½ cups good-tasting vegetable (or chicken) stock	4 cloves garlic, minced	Black pepper to taste
	1 cup Arborio rice	2–3 tablespoons butter
1½ cups water	¾ cup dry white wine	¼ cup freshly grated Parmesan,
1 tablespoon olive oil or butter	(or sub more stock)	plus additional for garnish

In a covered medium saucepan, bring the beets, stock, and water to a boil. Cook at a gentle boil for 40–45 minutes until beets are fork-tender. Remove the beets and let cool, while keeping the cooking liquid at a gentle simmer. When beets are cool enough to handle, peel off skins by rubbing with your hands or a kitchen towel, then grate using a box grater or food processor, or finely chop.

In a wide saucepan or Dutch oven over medium heat, warm the olive oil. Add the onion and cook 5 minutes, stirring occasionally, until starting to soften. Add the garlic, stir, and cook another minute.

Add the rice, stirring to coat, and cook 2–3 minutes. Add the wine (or additional stock) and bring to a simmer, stirring, about 2 minutes, until most of the liquid is absorbed.

Add a ladleful of the simmering beet stock, stirring frequently for about 1 minute until mostly absorbed. You will know when it is time to add more stock when you draw a line across the bottom of your pan with a wooden spoon. If you can still see the bottom of the pan by the time you finish drawing your line, then the risotto is ready for more liquid. If the rice rushes back immediately to fill the void left by the spoon, it needs to cook a bit longer before adding more liquid. After adding 3 ladles of stock, stir in the grated beets. Continue ladling and stirring for 18–20 minutes until the rice is al dente. You may not use all the stock.

When rice is cooked, immediately stir in salt, pepper, butter, and Parmesan cheese to taste. Stir until melted and fully incorporated. Serve, garnishing with more freshly grated Parmesan, if desired.

Serves four to six.

BERRIES

SN'T THIS WHAT we've all been waiting for? The day the first berries appear in the markets may be the single most significant factor that makes Minnesota winters bearable. Whether you come for a small box (or three) to munch on or a big flat of berries for freezing and preserving, the farmers market is a terrific place to pick up good-quality berries economically.

There's nothing wrong with expecting no more from your berries than great flavor when eaten straight out of hand, but once you've had your fill that way, you start thinking of dessert and breakfast uses: pies, cobblers, quick breads, preserves, jellies, and jams. And then, having run through the sweets, you should start thinking about savories. A tart berry sauce, its flavor heightened with balsamic vinegar, pairs nicely with roasts or can be spread on sandwiches with cured meats. Rich, meaty salmon is a classic choice for a berry sauce or chutney. Salads taste a little fresher and sweeter with a handful of berries thrown in, especially ones with sharp cheeses. Berries have an unexpected love for spice, from hot peppers to smoky paprika.

Strawberries, raspberries, and blackberries are familiar enough, but at Minnesota farmers markets you're also likely to find gooseberries and currants. Gooseberries range from spherical to rugby ball–shaped, from the size of the tip of your pinky to the tip of your thumb. They are smooth and striped, light green when immature and pink (and much sweeter) when ripe. They're often picked green, however, to keep ahead of the birds that love them, so green gooseberry recipes—especially pies and jam— are particularly popular. Sliced in half and tossed with salty feta and honey is a great way to enjoy them.

Black, red, and white currants are popular in northern Europe and familiar to many Minnesota country grandmothers. The rest of us may know currants best in their

WHEN TO FIND IT

Strawberries:
early to mid-June
Raspberries:
mid- to late June
**Currants, red,
black, and white:**
late June through
early July
Gooseberries:
late June through
early July
Blackberries:
July
Blueberries:
July through early August

1. Red currants and blueberries. 2. Strawberries. 3. Blackberries.

dried form. Red currants are smaller and more tart, while black currants are larger and have a rich and mildly astringent flavor. White currants (sometimes pinkish) are the sweetest and mildest of the three. Even those who love the flavors best are unlikely to just pop currants in their mouths like blueberries (at least not many of them). But currants make terrific jams and sauces and black currant juice is a positively delicious flavor. Because currants are less sweet than other berries, they are among the easiest to use in savory dishes.

Most berries need to be eaten the same day you buy them or the next. There is so much moisture in them that mold sets in quickly. Blueberries, currants, and gooseberries will keep a few days longer. Do wash your berries, but not until right before you intend to eat them or cook with them.

To freeze most berries, wash and stem them (remove the hulls of strawberries). Then spread them in a single layer, touching each other as little as possible, on a baking sheet or plate and put them in the freezer. When they're hard, transfer them to a plastic bag or other container. They'll keep for about three months in the freezer.

The exceptions are blueberries, currants, and gooseberries, which aren't moist enough to stick together when they freeze. Carol Whitcomb of J. Q. Fruit Farm and Orchard in Princeton puts fresh blueberries in an empty plastic ice cream bucket and sticks that in the freezer. When she's ready to bake, she just scoops out what she needs. Or, she says, she scoops out some frozen blueberries and pours a little half and half or cream over them for an instant dessert.

Making fruit preserves is as easy as cooking down clean berries with an equal amount of sugar by weight. Boil this mixture until it reaches 220 degrees F (this is the gelling point of sugar at Minnesota's altitude) or until it mounds up when you scoop it out with a cold spoon. This will keep in the fridge for a couple of weeks or in the freezer for three months, or you can preserve it in jars using your preferred canning method.

BLUEBERRY CORNMEAL SPOONBREAD

By Dorothy Stainbrook

Dorothy Stainbrook grows organic blueberries and tomatoes at Heath Glen farm in Forest Lake. She sells these at number of Twin Cities area farmers markets, along with her creative, award-winning preserves. She particularly enjoys finding savory uses for her fruit.

Stainbrook's spoonbread recipe draws equally on her Minnesota farm and her southern roots. "I was born in Alabama and grew up with a quintessential southern belle mother who loved her sweet potatoes and hush puppies," she says. "Her raison d'être was to make other people happy, especially family, and especially with food. As I have grown older I find myself drawn to southern cooking and to her stories of what she ate on her farm in Louisiana. Using blueberries from my Minnesota farm in a dish that honors her Louisiana farm experience was a joy to develop.

"Spoonbread is a traditional southern favorite and is something of a cross between a corn pudding, a cornbread, and a soufflé. Texture is all-important in a proper spoonbread. I went for a soft, sweet cornbread that you really can eat with a spoon, but holds it shape as a bread also."

Note: If you do not have self-rising cornmeal, use regular cornmeal (the finer the better) and add 1 tablespoon baking powder.

1 ¼ cups buttermilk (can use nonfat milk if desired)

½ cup brown sugar

¾ cup yellow cornmeal, self-rising

½ teaspoon kosher salt

2 tablespoons butter, unsalted

1 teaspoon vanilla

½ teaspoon 5-spice powder

½ teaspoon cinnamon

4 large eggs, yolks and whites separated

2 tablespoons heavy cream

¼ cup sugar

2 cups blueberries, fresh or frozen

Preheat oven to 375°F. Coat an 8x8" pan (or a 2-quart round dish, an 8x10" oval gratin dish, or individual ramekins) with butter or cooking spray.

In a saucepan, bring buttermilk and brown sugar to a low boil over medium-high heat. When the buttermilk begins to bubble around the edges of the pan, slowly whisk in the cornmeal and salt. Turn down the heat and stir with the whisk until thick (about 3 minutes, but time depends on your cornmeal). Mixture should be mushy and thick. Remove from heat and whisk in the butter, vanilla, and spices.

Whisk egg yolks in a separate bowl and add to the warm cornmeal mixture, whisking constantly so the eggs will not scramble. Add in the cream, whisking until smooth and well blended.

Beat egg whites in a stand mixer on high speed until soft peaks form. Gradually sprinkle in sugar, continuing to beat until soft glossy peaks form.

Gently fold the egg whites into the cornmeal mixture. Fold in blueberries. Spoon batter into buttered baking dish and top with a few blueberries.

Bake for 35–40 minutes (depends on the baking dish), until puffed and golden brown on top. Spoonbread will be firm around the edges, but wobbly in the center. Let cool for 20 minutes and serve with a dusting of powdered sugar or Greek yogurt.

SAVORY CREPES with SMOKED SALMON and BLUEBERRY CHUTNEY

By Dorothy Stainbrook

Here's what Stainbrook has to say about these delicious savory crepes: "Crepes are one of those dishes I have avoided, believing they were too fussy or complicated, but the versatility of crepes with sweet and savory fruit combinations finally lured me in, and I found that the intimidation was totally unnecessary. Crepes also freeze well, so spend a Sunday making up a batch to use at your convenience."

Crepes

Adapted from Jehnee Rains, previous pastry chef at Chez Panisse.

Crepe tips:

- Make the batter a day ahead in order to let it rest for 6 hours or overnight. This allows the gluten to develop and gives a much better flavor. This is not mandatory, but it's well worth it.
- The right pan will make life much easier. An inexpensive 8" omelet pan or crepe pan is what you need. Make sure it is nonstick.
- Straining the batter through a sieve will make your crepes light and perfect, even as it is an extra step.
- To freeze, layer wax paper between each crepe and place in a freezer bag as whole stacks.

1¼ cup flour	Set out eggs and rest of ingredients and bring to room temperature.
½ teaspoon sugar	In the bowl of a stand mixer with paddle attachment, slowly whisk
½ teaspoon salt	together flour, sugar, and salt.
2 cups milk	Combine the milk and butter in small bowl and heat to warm (not
¼ cup unsalted butter	boiling) in microwave. Set aside.
(½ stick), melted	Add eggs and oil to flour mix (slowly so flour doesn't fly all over).
3 eggs	Beat on low speed until blended (about 2 minutes). Slowly add
¾ tablespoon grape	the melted butter and milk mixture and beat on medium until
seed oil, or any	thoroughly combined.
unflavored oil	Pour batter through a fine sieve into another medium-size bowl,
½ cup beer, any	pressing any lumps through the sieve. Stir beer into the batter until
lighter lager beer	just combined (do not over mix!).
	Cover the batter and set aside for 6 hours or overnight.
	Makes 16–18 crepes.

Blueberry Chutney

1 tablespoon grape seed oil or olive oil	Heat oil in skillet over medium heat. Add onions and cook until tender, about 5 minutes. Add garlic, salt, thyme, and allspice, and stir until fragrant, about 30 seconds.
½ medium red onion, chopped	
2 garlic cloves, chopped	
¼ teaspoon kosher salt	
¼ teaspoon fresh thyme	Add blueberries, water, and vinegar and stir frequently until sauce thickens, mashing blueberries with a spoon while stirring to release juices.
¼ teaspoon ground allspice	
1 cup blueberries, fresh or frozen	
¼ cup water	
2 teaspoons balsamic vinegar	

Smoked Salmon Filling

6 ounces cream cheese, softened	Cream cheese and sour cream in mixer with paddle attachment until smooth. Stir in rest of ingredients and chill.
¼ cup sour cream	
1 lemon, zest and juice	
2 tablespoons chives, minced	
1 teaspoon horseradish, drained	
4 ounces smoked salmon	
Freshly ground pepper	

Putting It All Together

Spray 8" nonstick pan with cooking spray and heat over medium-high heat until smoking. Pour about ¼ to ⅓ cup batter into pan, swirling the pan to get the surface of the batter evenly distributed.

Cook about 1 minute on the first side, lifting up the edge occasionally to see if it is golden brown. When golden brown, flip crepe over and cook 15–30 seconds on the other side.

To flip: You can use your fingers, tongs, or spatula to flip the crepe. It will take you a couple of tries to see which method suits you best. Allow yourself to mess up the first couple of crepes until you settle on the flipping method that works best for you.

If you're serving immediately, cover the crepes with aluminum foil and keep warm in 200°F oven. For serving later, wrap them in plastic wrap in quantities intended for each use and slip them into a plastic bag. Refrigerate crepes for up to 3 days, or freeze them for up to 2 months.

To serve: There are many different ways of folding crepes. The easiest way is to place salmon and blueberry filling together on one side of the crepe and roll it up. It will end up long and skinny and you can serve more of the chutney on top or on the side. You can also make a triangle fold, where you place fillings on half of the crepe and fold the crepe over in half, then fold in half again.

BROCCOLI and CAULIFLOWER

BOTH BROCCOLI AND CAULIFLOWER are such familiar staples that we might walk right past them in the market, looking for something more unusual or trendier. That's a shame, because there's a reason these veggies are staples: They are versatile and hearty and go well with just about anything you might serve on a summer plate.

They are also two vegetables that many people remember staring down at dinnertime, willing the mushy florets and tough stems to disappear on their own, or at least before Mom and Dad noticed they weren't eating any of them. It's such a shame that boiled or steamed were most people's introduction to broccoli and cauliflower. Boiling and steaming really don't give these veggies a chance to show their best selves. (Boiled cauliflower, in fact, can develop a truly off-putting odor.)

Both broccoli and cauliflower are at their best when roasted. They develop delicious sweet, nutty flavors and get crunchy instead of mushy. To roast, toss the florets and chopped pieces of stem with just a little oil and salt and spread them on a pan, giving them plenty of room. Cook them at 400 degrees F until the tips are brown, about twenty minutes. If you just can't bear to heat up the oven on a hot summer day, thread florets on skewers, coat them in just a little oil, and cook them on a hot grill. Cauliflower, especially, likes a hit of lemon or orange zest after roasting.

Another key to enjoying broccoli is to eat the whole head—or nearly all of it. The stem can be the juiciest, best part of the vegetable. First, remove the florets. Then chop off the toughest inch or so at the base of the stem. (At this point, if you see that the stem is hollow or woody, it's time to give up on it and focus on the florets.) Peel the stem with a sharp knife, cutting away the outer eighth of an inch or so (better to take off too much than too little). Or do it the quick and dirty way: Place the stem on a

WHEN TO FIND IT

Broccoli is available for most of the market season, but it is at its peak in June and early July, before it gets too hot, and after the heat subsides, around the end of September.
Cauliflower is a late-season vegetable, best from late September through early November.

✸
Broccoli and cauliflower are at their best when roasted.

cutting board and cut away four sides to make a rectangular prism. Then slice the stem lengthwise or diagonally or cut it into fat cubes.

To prepare cauliflower, remove the leaves and hold the whole head upside down so you can cut out the tough core with a paring knife. You can separate the florets at this point. (The smaller the pieces, the more nicely they'll roast.) Or slice the whole head into fat "steaks." The flat surfaces will mean even more great roasted flavor.

If you must boil cauliflower, boil it until it is quite soft and then puree it with a little olive oil in the blender or food processor. Some people serve this as ersatz mashed potatoes, but it's really a nice side dish in its own right. Raw cauliflower can also be pulsed in the food processor until it is the consistency of rice, boiled briefly, and then served as a side in place of rice.

At the market, you may see some of broccoli's and cauliflower's kookier cousins, including purple varieties. Then there's Romanesco, which looks like a mysterious microscopic organism magnified hundreds of times, or like a computer illustration of fractal geometry. It is light green with protruding conical points that get smaller from the center to the edges. Its flavor is similar to cauliflower and you can cook it in all the same ways.

Broccoli raab or rapini is actually more closely related to turnips than to broccoli, but it looks like baby heads of broccoli with lots of fat leaves. You eat the whole thing, leaves, stems, and all (and if there are little yellow buds, those too). Rapini can be quite bitter: In fact, that's what it's prized for. To reduce the bitterness, blanche it in a pot with plenty of salted water before cooking it in some olive oil on the stovetop.

KNOCK-YOUR-SOCKS-OFF CAULIFLOWER SOUP

By Claudine Arndt

Claudine Arndt, who works with Minnesota Cooks and runs her own health coaching business, Wellness with Claudine, admits that she doesn't really love cauliflower. "You don't have to like everything," she says, "but I try to eat in season and the bulk of our produce comes from a CSA. The only way I ate cauliflower growing up was raw or boiled. So I became determined to find a way to like it." And this soup has won over many cauliflower converts.

1 tablespoon olive oil

1 tablespoon butter, or
    additional olive oil

1 yellow onion, chopped

2 leeks, white part only, washed
    thoroughly and chopped

1–2 cloves garlic, minced

2 heads cauliflower,
    roughly chopped

1 quart chicken broth

¾ cup coconut milk (or organic
    heavy whipping cream)

2 medium carrots, scrubbed
    and shredded

1 teaspoon dried parsley or
    4 tablespoons fresh parsley,
    chopped

Salt and freshly ground pepper,
    to taste

Heat olive oil and butter in a large saucepan over medium-low heat. Add onion, leek, and garlic, and cook until onion and leek are almost transparent. Add chopped cauliflower and broth. Bring to a low simmer and cook until the cauliflower is barely tender, breaking the cauliflower florets into small pieces as you occasionally stir the soup. When cauliflower is cooked to desired consistency (about 8–10 minutes), add coconut milk, shredded carrot, and parsley. Stir to combine and simmer an additional 3 minutes to soften the carrot slightly. Add more broth, if necessary. Season with salt and pepper, to taste.

Notes: If you like pureed soups, you can blend this soup prior to adding the shredded carrots and parsley. You can also stir in 2–4 ounces of heavy whipping cream at the end of cooking to add more body and richness to the soup.

Serves six to eight.

COULDN'T BE EASIER BROCCOLI SOUP

This soup tastes like the essence of broccoli, with a little sharp saltiness from the Parmesan.

2 medium heads broccoli,
    stems and crowns

1–2 Parmesan rinds

Water or mild-tasting
    chicken broth

¼ cup finely grated
    Parmesan or
    ½ cup half and half

Separate broccoli florets from stems. Peel stems, removing all tough woody parts. Chop florets and stems roughly and place in a medium pot with rinds and just enough water or broth to cover. Put the lid on, bring to a boil, reduce to a simmer, and cook for 20 minutes. Remove and discard rind.

Puree in batches in a standing blender or with a stick blender. Stir in Parmesan or half and half, or both if you're feeling decadent. If you don't use the Parmesan, taste and add salt as needed.

CAULIFLOWER TABOULI

Courtesy of the Mill City Farmers Market

The Mill City Farmers Market in downtown Minneapolis has been a favorite Saturday morning gathering spot for families and food-lovers since it opened in 2006. The market has a remarkable pedigree, founded by beloved Minnesota restaurateur Brenda Langton, of Spoonriver and the late, great Café Brenda.

The market regularly hosts chefs and farmers who demonstrate their favorite recipes, and market staff develop recipes, like this one, to share with shoppers.

1 head cauliflower
5 tablespoons olive oil, divided
Salt and pepper to taste
1 bunch parsley
1 large tomato
4 green onions
½ cucumber
Zest and juice of one lemon
Optional spices: cinnamon, nutmeg, cloves, and so on

Finely chop the cauliflower. (Pulsing in a food processor works well.) Pour about 1 tablespoon olive oil into a large sauté pan and heat over medium-high heat. Sauté the cauliflower with salt and pepper to taste. Allow to cool.

Chop parsley, tomato, green onion, and cucumber to desired size. Mix cauliflower and vegetables in a large bowl. Add juice from one lemon and the remaining 4 tablespoons olive oil. Add lemon zest and optional spices to taste.

CABBAGE, BOK CHOY, and BRUSSELS SPROUTS

CRAVING SOMETHING SWEET, green, and crunchy in the dark depths of winter? Don't overlook the humble cabbage.

We tend to eat cabbage raw in the summer in creamy and vinegary cole slaws and cooked in the winter. But when local lettuce is long gone from the farmers markets, you can still put a salad on the table if you have a head of cabbage in the crisper and some really good olive oil and vinegar.

Cabbage seems to be nearly ubiquitous in world cuisines: from sauerkraut to kimchi, from stuffed cabbage rolls (in Eastern Europe, Italy, and Spain) to sweet, yeasty rolls stuffed with cabbage (in Eastern Europe) to cabbage dumplings (all over Asia).

You'll find three basic types of cabbage in the market: familiar head cabbage in green and red; Savoy cabbage, which is looser, lighter, crinklier, and has a mild, mustardy flavor; and Napa cabbage, which has a loose elongated head, fading from green at the tips to white at the base. Of the three, head cabbage is by far the sweetest. There's really no difference in flavor between red and green cabbage.

The tighter the head, the longer cabbage will keep in the fridge: four to six weeks. Though cabbage resists going off, its flavor does change, from sweet and fresh to starchy and a little bitter. When cabbage is chopped or cooked, that distinctive cabbage-y skunkiness emerges. Cabbage contains enzymes and sulfides that are kept separate until the cell walls start to break down and allow them to combine. To reduce this, you can soak chopped or sliced cabbage in plenty of cold water if you're going to use it raw, or blanch it in plenty of boiling water if you're going to use it cooked.

As Old World cooks know, cabbage loves butter, which brings out a lovely nutty flavor. And it mixes

WHEN TO FIND IT

Baby bok choy appears in the markets in spring. This variety of cabbage can be found in the markets for most of the season, but it is at its best when the cool whether comes in early fall. **Brussels sprouts** are available late September through mid-November.

1. Cabbage. 2. Brussels sprouts. 3. Bok choy (also called Chinese cabbage).

surprisingly well with other dairy products, in creamy soups and béchamel sauces. Caraway and juniper seeds are tart balances to cabbage's natural sweetness. Apples and red cabbage are a classic pairing for a good reason: The acid in the apples (boosted by some vinegar, if needed) helps keep the whole dish from turning an unpleasant purple, as red cabbage tends to do when cooked.

At the market, look for tight, firm heads with some heft to them. Check the base of the heads for evidence that lots of outer leaves have been pulled off. Pulling off more than a few is one way to make an older cabbage look fresher and younger.

CABBAGE, BOK CHOY, and BRUSSELS SPROUTS 51

Both Napa cabbage and bok choy are sometimes called Chinese cabbage, although they are very different things. Bok choy is closely related to the turnip (they're all *Brassicas*) and has a distinctive, milky white base topped with fans of darker green leaves. Baby bok choy (the size of your palm) are sweet and elegant on the plate, but bok choy doesn't lose flavor as it grows, so don't look down on the full-size plant (about a foot long). Baby bok choy can be cooked whole, but with larger bok choy you need to slice the leaves and white stems separately and give the stems a few extra minutes head start in the pan. Bok choy is packed with water, so you need to cook it quickly on fairly high heat to keep that liquid from flooding out into your dish. Blanching bok choy in plenty of salted water (don't forget the quick plunge in ice water to stop the cooking) will reduce bitterness and ensure even cooking.

Bok choy doesn't keep nearly as long as its cabbage cousins: Use it up within a week.

Poor Brussels sprouts are the butt of many jokes. They're everybody's favorite vegetable to hate, which is entirely understandable if the only Brussels sprouts you've tasted are old and boiled into submission. Freshly picked—as in, that very day or as close to it as you can get—Brussels sprouts are something else altogether. They are sweet and fresh tasting and need little more than a quick sauté in a hot pan. (Cut off the stem ends and slice them in half. The flat surface will brown nicely in the pan.) Like cabbage, fresh Brussels sprouts can be served raw. Shaved into thin shreds, they make a lovely slaw.

These little mini cabbage heads will keep—as in, not rot—for weeks in a plastic bag in the fridge, but their sugars start converting into starches immediately and the descent from sweet and fresh toward that infamous cabbaginess is quick. If you need convincing, get your hands on some freshly picked Brussels sprouts and eat some today and some in a couple of days. You will notice the difference.

If your Brussels sprouts are older or very big, they are good candidates for long, slow cook. See the opposite page for a way to dress them up.

At the market, look for sprouts that are still attached to the stalk. This delays (though just a bit) the conversion of sugars into starches. It's also a faster way to harvest, so they're more likely to be fresh. But don't make any assumptions: Ask the farmer when the sprouts were picked. If the answer is, "This morning," then rush those sprouts home and enjoy them right away.

FANCY BRUSSELS SPROUTS

One way to cook Brussels sprouts is quickly and lightly over high heat. The other way is to cook the heck out of them until they get almost melly. This slightly over-the-top recipe goes the second way.

8 ounces bacon, chopped

1 cup thinly sliced shallots

1½ pounds Brussels sprouts, sliced in half

3 sprigs fresh thyme or 1 teaspoon dried thyme

½ cup slivered almonds

½ cup dried currants or raisins

½ cup white wine

Cook bacon and shallots in a large sauté pan over medium heat until bacon is crispy and shallots are brown. Drain off most but not all of the grease. Add sprouts and turn up heat; cook until sprouts have started to brown.

Add remaining ingredients and cover. Cook over medium-low heat 30 minutes, until sprouts are quite tender. Remove lid and turn up the heat and cook, stirring often, until any remaining liquid has boiled off.

ZUPPA VALDOSTANA

By Andrew Zimmern. Originally published in Andrew Zimmern's Kitchen Adventures *at foodandwine.com.*

Andrew Zimmern may be best known around the country as the guy who eats bugs and just about anything else on the Travel Channel's "Bizarre Foods," but here in Minnesota he's known as a chef and a tireless promoter of real, local food. Zimmern describes this as "my interpretation of a soup my dad and I had in the early '70s in the Italian Alps. In winter, local families would cook food all day, offering dishes in trencherman-size portions to hungry skiers seeking a seat by a fire and a hearty meal." It's almost hard to believe that something this filling and flavorful can star the humble cabbage.

2 tablespoons extra-virgin olive oil

5 pounds meaty beef shanks, cut 1½" thick

Salt

Freshly ground pepper

2 flat-leaf parsley sprigs

2 thyme sprigs

1 rosemary sprig

1 bay leaf, tied in a cheesecloth bundle with the parsley, thyme, and rosemary

½ pound white mushrooms, stems discarded and thinly sliced

1 small onion, finely diced

1 large carrot, cut into ¼" dice

2 celery ribs, cut into ¼" dice

2 large tomatoes, peeled and cut into ½" dice

2 cups dry red wine

One 2-pound head of savoy cabbage, cored and coarsely chopped

4 tablespoons unsalted butter

1 baguette, sliced crosswise ½" thick

½ pound Gruyere cheese, shredded

Preheat the oven to 325°F. In a large Dutch oven, heat the olive oil until shimmering. Season the beef shanks with salt and pepper and brown them in the oil over moderately high heat, about 2½ minutes per side. Transfer the shanks to a plate.

Add the herb bundle to the pot along with the mushrooms, onion, carrot, and celery. Cook, stirring, until the vegetables begin to soften, about 2 minutes. Add the tomatoes and wine, and scrape to dislodge any browned bits stuck to the bottom of the pot. Bring to a boil and simmer for 2 minutes. Return the shanks to the pot, add 10 cups of water, and bring to a boil. Transfer the casserole to the oven and braise until the meat is very tender, about 2 hours. Let cool slightly.

When the meat is cool enough to handle, pull the meat from the bones and return it to the pot. Discard the bones, cartilage, and fat. Cover the stew and refrigerate overnight.

Bring a large pot of salted water to a boil. Add the cabbage and blanch for 1 minute; drain well.

Discard the fat that has solidified on the top of the stew. Rewarm the stew, then strain the broth into another large pot; reserve the meat and vegetables. Bring the broth to a simmer and add the cabbage. Cover and simmer over moderate heat until the cabbage is very tender, about 1 hour. Add the reserved meat and vegetables, season with salt and pepper and remove from the heat.

Preheat the oven to 350°F. In a large skillet, melt 2 tablespoons of the butter over moderate heat. Add half of the baguette slices in a single layer and toast until golden brown, about 1 minute per side. Wipe out the skillet and repeat with the remaining 2 tablespoons of butter and the remaining baguette slices.

Line the bottom of a clean casserole or individual ovenproof bowls with half of the baguette toasts. Top with half of the Gruyere and fill with the stew. Cover with the remaining toasts and then with the remaining cheese. Transfer carefully to the oven and bake until the cheese is golden and bubbling, about 20 to 45 minutes. Serve hot.

Serves 10.

CARROTS, PARSNIPS, and SALSIFY

S THERE A MORE classic farmers market sight than bunches of carrots, stacked like firewood and ready to be snapped up by nearly every passing shopper? Carrots are easy to love: sweet, familiar, earthy, easy to eat, and easy to cook. In fact, they're so easy to slice up for lunches and snacks that we might even forget how versatile they can be in the kitchen.

Carrots are culinary chameleons that change their flavors based on how you cook them. Nearly every cuisine in the world has adopted carrots, and with good reason: They are friendly with a huge range of flavors, from mint and ginger, which play up their sweetness, to thyme, rosemary, coriander, and cumin, which play up their earthiness.

Simmering carrots low and slow—as in the Carrots Vichy recipe on page 57, in a soup, or in a stew—also emphasizes their sweet flavors, while roasting them or sautéing on high heat brings out their earthy notes. (No matter which of the carrot's personalities you prefer, there's really no need to boil the life out of a poor carrot, and steaming doesn't really allow carrots to show their full range of charms, either.)

Carrots are welcome, but almost unexpected, additions to stir-fries and to risotto. They sweeten meat stews and give broths and stocks a little extra oomph. They are, with little exaggeration, transcendent when roasted. In fact, if you find little bunches of young, sweet, skinny carrots in the early summer, buy two, because the first you will not be able to resist polishing off while still raw, and you'll want to keep the other on hand to roast, whole, in olive oil and salt, at 400 degrees F until blistery brown on the outside.

WHEN TO FIND IT

Baby carrots—true young carrots, not large ones whittled down by machine—are available from growers with hoop houses or other passive solar operations in the early summer and mature carrots should be easy to find for most of the market season. **Parsnips** are generally harvested after the first frost and are often available in the early spring from growers who have overwintered them. **Salsify** is harvested after the first frost.

❋

1. Multicolored carrots. 2. Parsnips.

As you keep buying carrots throughout the market season, you'll notice a change in the flavor. Nearly every farmer and cook agrees: Carrots taste better, almost sugary sweet, after a few frosts. They are, of course, usually pretty fat by this time but should not be woody. These late-season carrots are especially nice for juicing.

When you're inspecting carrots at the market, a little fresh dirt still clinging to them is a good thing. It's a marker of how fresh the carrots are and shows that they have not been roughly washed. Bunches of multicolored carrots are beautiful, for sure, and something you can't find in most grocery stores, but the yellow, white, and purple carrots don't taste any different from their orange cousins.

Early in the season, look for carrots with the tops still on. Carrot tops are also a marker of freshness, but they are more than just window-dressing: They are actually tasty to eat. (Late-season carrots will not have tops, as they will have died off in the frost.) Carrot tops are pleasantly grassy and bitter and a little tough, but will soften up in a vinaigrette dressing. A simple pesto with garlic, your favorite nuts, olive oil, and parmesan is another easy way to serve them. You can also braise them like spinach, but it often takes more than a bunch to make a meal of them this way.

There's no reason to peel fresh carrots that come from the farmers market, but do give them a good scrub with a vegetable brush or a rough washcloth just before cooking or eating. With their tops removed, carrots will keep for a month in a plastic bag in the fridge. Tops will keep about a week when stored separately.

Parsnips look like long white carrots, usually with a more dramatic taper toward the end. Although they are not the most familiar of root vegetables, they have a club of loyal aficionados who get positively giddy when they see them in the market. (Lucky for those folks, they get two chances to enjoy fresh parsnips: in the early spring and late fall.)

What those aficionados love is the parsnip's peppery, rich, earthy flavor. They are often roasted, but braising—browning followed by slow, moist heat—is even better for parsnips, as they don't contain as much moisture as many other vegetables and are prone to drying out. Parsnips are a perfect addition to a roast or a stew and make a delicious pureed soup.

Unlike carrots, parsnips are rarely eaten raw. They're just too tough to chomp directly into like Bugs Bunny, but they can be grated or shaved into salads. Parsnips can also be substituted for carrots in cakes and other baked goods, but because they are drier and cook more slowly, they will alter the texture as well as the flavor.

Peel parsnips before cooking. If there is a dramatic difference in thickness between the thin end and the thick end, as there often is, consider cooking the thin parts separately.

At the market, look for relatively firm parsnips. They are naturally tougher and more rubbery than carrots and will not snap the way carrots do. Parsnip tops are not only inedible; they actually contain a potent skin irritant, and so you should never see parsnips sold with the tops attached. Parsnips will keep in a plastic bag in the fridge for about a month.

There's one more carrot lookalike in the market: salsify. Salsify is white like a parsnip, but shaggy, with lots of little side roots. Both the tops and the roots are edible—raw when young and cooked when bigger and tougher. Some say salsify tastes like oyster, others like artichoke or even mushrooms. Sauté or roast the roots with a little olive oil.

CARROTS VICHY
By Sue Zelickson

If it's food-related in Minnesota, Sue Zelickson probably knows something about it and may have even had a hand in bringing it to life. The James Beard Award–winner founded both the organization Women Who Really Cook and the Kids' Café program for disadvantaged families, as well as the Minnesota Monthly Food and Wine Show and the Charlie Awards. Zelickson doesn't have much time to cook and entertain these days, but she always loves recipes that look and taste good.

8 to 10 fresh, young carrots
¼ cup butter (less if desired)
1 tablespoon water
1 teaspoon granulated or
    brown sugar
½ teaspoon salt
⅛ teaspoon freshly ground
    black pepper
Minced fresh parsley

Scrape carrots with a vegetable peeler and slice each one in half lengthwise, then slice each half into ⅛" strips. Melt butter in medium pan, then add water and the carrots. Cover tightly and cook over low heat for 15 to 20 minutes or until carrots are still a bit crunchy. Add sugar, salt, and pepper. Taste for seasoning. Sprinkle with minced parsley and serve at once.

Serves six.

GINGER-CARROT BISQUE

By Gregory Oja

Gregory Oja farms at the Maatila and sells at the Bemidji Farmers Market. He uses high tunnels to coax life out of the Minnesota soil as early as possible and specializes in early season vegetables, such as snow peas, lettuce, spinach, kale, garlic, and herbs. And, of course, fresh young carrots.

¼ cup plus 2 tablespoons
  unsalted butter
2 pounds carrots, peeled
  and sliced ⅛" thick
2 large onions, chopped
1 tablespoon minced
  peeled fresh ginger
2 teaspoon grated orange peel
½ teaspoon ground coriander
5 cups chicken stock or water
1 cup half and half
½ cup minced fresh parsley

Melt butter in a heavy large saucepan over medium heat. Add carrots and onions. Cover saucepan and cook until vegetables begin to soften, stirring occasionally, about 15 minutes. Mix in ginger, orange peel, and coriander. Add 2 cups of stock. Reduce heat to medium-low. Cover pan and simmer soup until carrots are tender, about 30 minutes.

Puree soup in batches in a processor or blender. Add remaining 3 cups stock and half and half to soup. Season with salt and pepper. Ladle into bowls, sprinkle with parsley, and serve.

Makes 9–10 cups.
Serves 10.

CHERRIES

CHERRY SEASON IS so brief and so precious you'll want to mark it on your calendar. Block off all of June and plan to cruise the markets every chance you get. Once you find boxes of juicy cherries, snap them up. Don't count on being able to buy them next week—they might be gone.

These aren't the sweet cherries—that's your Bings and your Rainiers and the like—that you just pop in your mouth. Those don't grow well in Minnesota. More likely, what you'll find are sour cherries (also called tart cherries or pie cherries). For all but the most sour-loving palates, these are too tart to just eat out of hand. (But keep your eye out for one Minnesota-bred variety, the Mesabi, a cross between sweet and sour cherries.)

Sour cherries tend to be a little smaller than their sweet cousins. Many are also bright red, rather than deep maroon. They're called "pie cherries" because many pie recipes call for these. In fact, sour cherries are fantastic in all sorts of baked goods. Halve them, pit them, and toss them with a little sugar to coat and stir them into your favorite quick bread or scone recipe. Use about an equal weight of sugar (or less, if you've got a sour tooth), top with your favorite crumble or sweet biscuit topping and bake. Or take sour cherries, again with an equal weight of sugar, and cook it down until it is soft and spreadable, for simple cherry preserves. If you've got one, scrape out the insides of a vanilla pod. Cherries love rich flavors such as real vanilla and chocolate.

You can also squirrel summer cherries away for the long winter by preserving them in liquor: Put two cups of pitted cherries in a jar with a half cup of brown sugar and a cup of brandy, bourbon, or rum. Give it a shake and put it in the fridge. Use the cherries to top your ice cream and the liquor in your mixed drinks all winter long.

Sour cherries aren't destined exclusively for desserts, of course. In Persian cooking, the beloved dish *albaloo polow* is steamed rice with sour cherries. You can also cook down cherries, or their juice, with just a pinch of

WHEN TO FIND IT
Sour cherries ripen
in late June.

59

✳

Sour cherries (also called tart cherries or pie cherries) are too sour
to eat raw, but are delicious in pies, crumbles, and other baked goods.

sugar into a sauce, finish it with balsamic vinegar, and serve it over meats. Throw a few sour cherries in with your brisket or pot roast to add a layer of rich, tart flavor.

Cherries freeze well. Just throw them in a plastic bag and squeeze as much of the air out as you can. You can pit them first or you can take advantage of the fact that cherries are much easier to pit after they've been frozen. After you thaw them out, you'll be able to pinch each pit out of the soft flesh with just your thumb and forefinger. In fact, even if you're not planning on long-term storage, throwing the cherries in the freezer the day before you plan to cook with them will make pitting a lot easier.

At the market, look for firm, smooth cherries. Ask to taste one: It will be sour, of course, but this will help you decide whether you want to buy these cherries for sweet or savory dishes. Cherries will keep in the refrigerator for three to five days. Don't wash them until you are ready to use them.

SOUR CHERRY CHOCOLATE LOAF CAKE

This cake isn't pretty, but the combination of chocolate and cherries is divine.

1 cup softened unsalted butter
1 cup brown sugar
2 large eggs
1 teaspoon vanilla extract
4 ounces baking chocolate, melted and cooled
1⅓ cup all-purpose flour
½ teaspoon baking soda
½ teaspoon table salt
1 cup hot water
1 cup pitted sour cherries, fresh or frozen
½ cup white sugar

Preheat oven to 375°F. Grease and flour a 9x5" loaf pan. Cream butter and brown sugar. Add vanilla, then eggs, one at a time. Fold in melted chocolate.

Sift together flour, baking soda, and salt, and stir half of this into the batter. Stir in the water and then the remaining half of the flour.

Toss cherries with white sugar and fold them into the batter. Pour into the prepared baking pan. Bake 45 minutes, until firm in the center and allow to cool completely.

ALBALOO POLOW (PERSIAN CHERRY RICE)

This unexpected combination—a classic in Persian cuisine—will challenge your idea of where sour cherries belong on the dinner table.

6 cups long-grain rice,
 such as basmati
 or jasmine
¼ cup olive oil
2 cups pitted
 sour cherries,
 fresh or frozen
2 tablespoons butter,
 cut into small squares

Wash rice in cold water until water runs clear. Bring a large pot of salty water to a boil. Add washed rice and boil 6 minutes. Drain and rinse immediately, again with very cold water. Leave rice to drain.

Heat oil in a wide-bottomed saucepan (nonstick is best). Spoon half the rice into the pan and smooth it out. Spread cherries evenly over rice and dot with butter. Spoon and smooth remaining rice. Wrap a kitchen towel around the lid of the pan (it should fit tightly) and place the pan over low heat for 1½ to 2 hours. Cook until the rice smells nutty and you can sense a crunchy crust on the bottom when you slice a knife along the edge and lift gently. When it's done, invert the whole pan onto a large platter.

CHICKEN and TURKEY

THE FREEZER WITH the local chickens and turkeys might be a little hard to find at your market. That's because it's often the one swarmed with customers. Chicken is the most popular meat in America by a wide margin, not just at the grocery store but also at the market.

Meat, including poultry, costs more at the farmers market than it does at the grocery store, but the quality and flavor wins over plenty of converts.

Whole birds cost much less per pound, so it is worth it to learn how to cut up a bird. A pair of heavy-duty chicken shears are a useful tool. The fastest way to cook a whole chicken is to use those shears to cut out the back bone (save it in the freezer to make broth later) and, using the heels of your hands backed up by your full weight, press down the on bird to break the breastbone. Tuck the bird's wings up in its armpits. Heat the oven to 450 degrees F. Heat a large pan over medium-high heat on the stove with a little olive oil. Brown the whole bird, skin side down, for about seven minutes. Using two sets of tongs, flip the bird over and put the whole pan in the oven. Your bird is done when an instant-read thermometer in the thigh indicates 160 degrees F, which should take about thirty minutes. It's almost faster than running out for rotisserie chicken.

But poultry parts do have their place. If you've got some chicken breasts or turkey tenders in the fridge, you are fifteen minutes from dinner: Season them well, pound them with a kitchen mallet to about one-quarter-inch thick, and cook them over medium-high heat for a couple of minutes on each side. A squeeze of lemon and you are done.

Of course, chicken legs rolled generously in olive oil and seasonings (salt, pepper, and smoked paprika, for example) and roasted at 375 degrees F for about thirty minutes make a particularly comforting dinner.

At the market, look for a vendor who is eager to talk about his or her farm and birds and how they are raised. Ask about how much time the birds spend outside and

WHEN TO FIND IT

Frozen **chicken** and **turkey** are likely to be available throughout the market season.

✱

If you buy turkey or chicken at the farmers market, you can talk to the grower to find out where the birds were raised.

what they eat. Chickens (unlike most other farm animals) do eat grain naturally, but they also eat grass and all the tasty bugs and such that live in the grass.

Thaw poultry overnight (twenty-four hours or longer for whole birds or turkey breasts) in the fridge. Don't attempt to speed up the process in the microwave or with hot water. Use fresh or thawed meat within three to five days. Frozen poultry will keep for three to six months in the freezer or six to twelve months in the deep freeze.

WARMING TURKEY CASSOULET

By Jane Peterson

The third generation of Petersons are now farming at Peterson Turkey Farm in Cannon Falls. Since the beginning, the Petersons have raised their turkeys "on range," meaning they move them to fresh pasture every week. If you stop by the Ferndale Market—where you can buy a full range of Minnesota products, from turkey to meat to wild rice to produce—you'll probably see the flecks of white and red out among the grass.

This turkey cassoulet—made, naturally, with Ferndale turkeys—is Peterson's American take on the classic French winter casserole.

3 large turkey thighs

2 tablespoons canola or olive oil

Poultry seasoning, salt, and pepper to taste

2½ to 3 cups favorite winter vegetables, cut in large chunks (celery, carrots, parsnips, onion)

1 large apple, cored and sliced

1 cup chicken broth or water

⅓ cup wine (red or white)

⅓ cup barbecue sauce

Brown turkey lightly in oil on both sides. When turning to second side, sprinkle browned side with poultry seasoning, salt, and pepper. Season second side when lightly browned. Place vegetables and half the apple slices in bottom of 3½–4-quart (or larger) slow cooker and season lightly with salt and pepper. Pour in the broth and wine. Place turkey and the rest of the apple slices on top of vegetables and pour barbeque sauce over the top of the turkey. Cover and cook on low for about 6 to 8 hours.

CREAMY CHICKEN SOUP with BABY PEAS and CARROTS

By Gregory Oja

This recipe uses many of the fresh early-season vegetables Gregory Oja grows and sells at the Bemidji Area Farmers Market. It can also be made with fresh chicken (see below). Try it also with 1 teaspoon of smoked paprika in place of the curry powder.

2 tablespoons unsalted butter

2 large carrots, thinly sliced

1 leek, white and tender green parts, halved lengthwise and thinly sliced

1 rotisserie chicken, dark meat and white meat pulled and coarsely shredded separately (3 cups total)

½ teaspoon mild curry powder

4 cups chicken stock or low-sodium broth

3 ounces crustless peasant or country white bread, cut into 1" cubes (2¼ cups)

½ cup half and half

1 cup frozen baby peas

1 tablespoon finely chopped flat-leaf parsley

Salt and freshly ground white pepper

In a medium saucepan, melt the butter. Add the carrots and leek and cook over moderate heat, stirring, until slightly softened, about 4 minutes. Add the dark meat and curry powder and cook, stirring, for 1 minute. Add 3 cups of the stock and season with salt and white pepper. Simmer over moderate heat until the vegetables are tender, about 5 minutes.

Meanwhile, in a blender, puree the bread with the remaining 1 cup of stock and the half and half. Stir the puree into the soup along with the peas and simmer over low heat until thickened, about 8 minutes. Add the white meat and cook just until heated through, 2 to 3 minutes. Stir in the parsley and serve right away.

Variation with Fresh Chicken

Place one whole fresh chicken in a large stockpot with enough water to cover. Bring to a boil, skim off any foam that comes to the top. Reduce heat and cook at a bare simmer for 1 hour. Allow chicken to cool in pot to just above room temperature.

Remove chicken from pot. Strain broth through cheesecloth to remove any residue. Use hands to remove white and dark meat from chicken, discarding skin, bones, and so on.

Proceed as above, using the chicken meat and four cups of the broth.

CORN and CORNMEAL

FRESH SWEET CORN can get your hopes up and deliver deep disappointment like no other vegetable. When it is good, it is very, very good, like the perfect summer evening. And when it lets us down, it feels like the entire food landscape has shifted out from under us and we'll never taste the foods of our childhood again. That's the nature of sweet corn: It inspires melodrama.

The sugars in corn start to turn starchy the moment it's picked. That's why the old advice (only partially in jest) used to be to put the pot of water on to boil before you go out to pick the corn for dinner. To combat this, commercial corn has been bred to be many times sweeter than it used to be and to retain that sweetness over a longer period of time. The cost of this miraculous new property (which translates into its ability to be shipped) is flavor. The sweetness replaced the corn flavor of corn.

This may be why people who are content to do 99 percent of their weekly shopping at a large grocery store will swing by the farmers market just for sweet corn or, even more likely, screech to a halt and back up dangerously along a country road to get a dozen ears from the back of a pickup.

At the market (or that pickup truck), you want to ask when the farmer picked the corn. If he or she is smart, the answer will be "this morning." You can tell whether this is true by inspecting the husks and the tassels. You want moist, green husks and soft, golden tassels. Pull the husk back and look for signs of rot at the tip of the ear, but don't worry if not all of the kernels at the tip are fully developed. Pick off a kernel and pop one in your mouth. It should be sweet and creamy. (After all that, be sure to buy that particular ear.)

Some people have strong preferences about yellow versus white corn, but that the color of the kernels has nothing to do with the flavor, beyond indicating a particular variety.

WHEN TO FIND IT

Corn will appear in the market in August and be gone by early September. Fresh **cornmeal** is likely to be available in the spring, but some farmers may have it available all season long.

The faster you can get an ear of sweet corn from the field to your table, the better it will taste.

When corn is young and fresh, it barely needs to be cooked. Just two to three minutes in salted boiling water will do the trick. If your corn is older, cook it longer and try adding a tablespoon or so of honey to the cooking water to boost the sweetness.

Grilling corn is a good way to coax another layer of flavor out of it. There are two schools of thought here: You can roast it in the husk or with the husk removed. If you do the former, you need to soak the ears for thirty minutes or so, so that they don't catch on fire. You'll get a subtler smoky flavor this way than if the kernels are directly over the fire and allowed to brown.

To cut the kernels off the cob, stand the cob vertically on a cutting board (it's a good idea to put the cutting board inside a roasting pan or something else to contain the occasional flying kernel) and run the knife down the side. Then, turn the knife around so that the dull side is facing the cob and run it down again. This "milks" the cob, popping the last bit of starch out of each little kernel. Fresh, raw corn kernels are excellent toasted in a little butter on a hot frying pan for those days when you have had enough corn on the cob.

Leftover cobs usually go right into the trash or onto the compost pile, but Bea Westerberg of the Hastings Farmers Market gets every last bit of goodness out of them by making a corn stock. She simmers them with just enough water to cover them, in a covered pan, for about an hour. Then she strains the cobs and cooks down the liquid (uncovered) until it is reduced by about half. This freezes well, she says, and "adds an awesome flavor to corn and other vegetable soups."

Corn, as we said, simply doesn't retain its flavor long, but if you're not going to cook it today, wrap it tightly in plastic—some people recommend wrapping each ear individually—and store it in the refrigerator. It will keep—as in, not go bad—for a week or so, but it just won't taste the same.

Cornmeal is ground from flour corn, rather than sweet corn. Flour corn can be white, yellow, blue, red, or multicolored. At the market, look for freshly ground, whole-grain cornmeal, which will include the germ and the hull (parts that are typically removed from commercial cornmeal). This means it has more fiber, more fat, and more flavor. It also means it can spoil, so you'll need to keep it in the refrigerator. You can use it in all your favorite recipes for cornmeal without changing anything. You can also cook it on its own to make polenta, cornmeal mush, or mamaliga. It will be heavenly. Simmer it slowly in four to five times the amount of water, stirring often, for about forty-five minutes.

SWEET CORN SOUP

By Atina Diffley

For more than two decades, Atina Diffley and her husband, Martin, farmed at Gardens of Eagan, an organic farm on the edge of the Twin Cities metro area. These days, she teaches what she has learned about caring for the soil to other farmers. She is the author of the memoir *Turn Here, Sweet Corn*, and this simple, powerful recipe echoes her personality and her wisdom.

1½ cups leeks, chopped	Cook leeks in olive oil or butter over medium heat until soft. Add corn and vegetable stock and simmer for 10–15 minutes or until the corn is tender.
1 tablespoon olive oil or butter	
½ cup vegetable stock	
4 cups corn, cut from the cob (about 4 ears)	Puree in food processor or blender until smooth. Return the soup to the pan; add cream. Bring to a gentle simmer and cook for about 5 minutes. Season with salt, white pepper, and paprika.
½ cup heavy cream	
Salt, pepper, and paprika to taste	Garnish with corn, red pepper, parsley, or chopped onion; sprinkle lemon juice on top.

SWEET CORN RELISH

By Lenny Russo

Lenny Russo was serving local, sustainable food long before it was cool. He serves this relish with a grilled Minnesota pork loin brushed with rosemary and lavender. You may balk at the two types of oil, but each brings a distinctive flavor to the dish.

4 ears sweet corn, shucked

¼ cup sweet onions, peeled and diced (⅛")

¼ cup green onions, bias sliced (⅛")

1 teaspoon fresh garlic, minced

2 tablespoons fresh rosemary, chopped

2 tablespoons apple cider vinegar

2 tablespoons grape seed oil

1 tablespoon walnut oil

1 tablespoon fine sea salt

½ tablespoon black pepper, freshly ground

Cut the corn kernels from the cobs and cook them in salted boiling water for 7 minutes. While the corn is cooking, dissolve the salt in the vinegar in a mixing bowl. Whisk in the oils. Strain the corn and add it along with the remaining ingredients to the mixing bowl. Blend well and set aside.

Makes about 4 cups.

CUCUMBERS

CUCUMBERS ARE MORE refreshing than flavorful, to be sure, but when you keep your eyes out for a little diversity, they can be surprisingly exciting as well.

Cucumbers come in a wide range of sizes and shapes, from the size of your thumb to the size of your forearm, from nearly perfect spheres to long, skinny spears. The kinds you're likely to find in Minnesota markets are garden cucumbers, with thick, smooth skins; English cucumbers, which are skinnier and seedless and have thinner skins; and pickling cucumbers, which have spiny ridges. Some growers may have the round varieties favored in parts of Asia.

When cucumbers are quite fat, they are likely to be pulpy or watery. The bigger a cucumber gets, the more developed its seeds are. To remove the seeds, cut the cucumber in half lengthwise and scoop them out in a long furrow with a spoon, or quarter it lengthwise and slice off the seeds diagonally.

Wash the skins thoroughly and if you don't know much about the grower's practices, consider removing the skin entirely because they are quite porous and will absorb toxins. Some people peel all cucumbers except the seedless, tender-skinned English variety, finding the skin too bitter. Others consider the skin the most flavorful part of a cucumber and enjoy it.

Most of us eat cucumbers raw and cold, but they're actually delicious cooked. You can add them to a stir-fry or sauté them on their own over medium-high or high heat. If your pan is too cool, they will get watery before they have a chance to cook. Cook them with some garlic and sesame oil, then toss them with a little soy sauce, rice vinegar, and sugar for an Asian-style room-temperature salad.

Cucumbers, sliced as thin or as thick as you like, can be made into quick refrigerator pickles with a brine of vinegar and salt, as well as sugar or spices, if you like. They're better the second day and will keep weeks in the fridge this way. (Discard them if they look cloudy or smell off in any way.)

WHEN TO FIND IT

Cucumbers are at the heart of the vegetable explosion in July and August, and you might see some stragglers in September.

You can make your cooked cucumbers, salad, or refrigerator pickles a little crispier by salting them first to remove excess water: Slice the cucumbers and toss with a teaspoon or so of kosher salt and leave them to drain in a colander for a half hour or so. Rinse to remove salt and drain all the water, then use them in your recipe.

At the market, look for cucumbers that are firm, relatively heavy, free of blemishes, and not too yellow. The stem end should feel firm. If you're buying a half-bushel for pickling, be sure to look beyond the top layer of cucumbers.

Dedicated picklers believe that the best pickles are made from cucumbers cut from the vine that very day. If you can't find them that fresh, chill them in a large bowl of very cold water for about an hour before pickling.

MARINATED CUCUMBERS

By Sue Zelickson

Award-winning food journalist and noted foodie (from long before anyone else was a foodie) Sue Zelickson notes that this is a marvelous side dish for salmon and seafood. You can peel the cucumber if you prefer.

6 cups sliced cucumbers	Mix all together. Marinate in refrigerator for 24 hours. Keeps for weeks.
1 cup sliced onions	
2 cups granulated sugar (less if desired)	
1 cup tarragon vinegar	
2 teaspoons mustard seed	
2 teaspoons salt (less if desired)	

CUCUMBER BUTTERMILK SOUP

By Kathy Zeman

Adapted from **Joy of Gardening Cookbook** *by Janet Ballantyne.*

Kathy Zeman and her brother, Nick, raise chickens, turkeys, geese, ducks, goats, pigs, sheep, and rabbits—as well as a full roster of vegetables—at Simple Harvest Farm Organics in Nerstrand. It is truly an omnivore's farm. She sells her eggs at the Riverwalk Market Fair in Northfield, along with goat's milk soap, wool, pottery, and more. She loves to make this soup almost entirely from her own ingredients and says it's a "great way to taste fresh cukes all year long."

6 cups peeled and chopped cucumbers

1/2 cup diced scallions

2 tablespoons minced fresh cilantro, mint, or dill

2 cups goat milk buttermilk

1 cup sour cream

3 tablespoons lemon juice

1 teaspoon salt

Combine all ingredients in a blender or food processor and process until smooth. Serve cold, garnished with grated cucumber or diced tomato if desired. This freezes and thaws very well.

Serves six.

✳

If you're buying a half-bushel of cucumbers for pickling, be sure to look under the top layer.

EGGPLANT

EGGPLANTS MAY BE the most seductively mysterious vegetables on the market tables and therefore the most likely to make it home and into the crisper, where they will languish without a plan for their use. There are the familiar fat, fleshy ones, so purple they're almost black. There are long, thin Asian eggplants that are either neon purple or delicate ivory. There are adorable little globe eggplants, firmer than their larger cousins and green, pink, white, or purple. All of them are so beautiful that you are likely to fill your market bag and worry about just what will become of them when you get home.

Think of eggplants as the tofu of the vegetable world: They're here for their texture, not their flavor, which is subtle, a little bitter, and something of an acquired taste.

Eggplants are like sponges, soaking up all the oil you give them, but without enough oil, they get unpleasantly dry and tough. This gives you, essentially, two choices: Sear them on high, high heat before they can start soaking up oil, or accept and capitalize on their absorbent properties and cook them low and slow, in plenty of oil, to make a decadent dip or stew.

In Asian cooking, eggplants are usually cooked quickly, on high heat. For stir-fries and the like, it's best to choose the long, skinny eggplants or the little globes, which are firmer than their Rubenesque cousins and not quite as absorbent. They carry the flavors of hot chili peppers and soy sauce with ease and lend a slightly bitter note to dishes already balanced with hot, sour, spicy, and sweet flavors.

In Mediterranean cooking, generally speaking, eggplant is cooked low and slow into stews with tomatoes, peppers, capers, and other bright flavors. There's Italian caponata, a spread made of stewed eggplant, onions, olives, raisins, capers, and sometimes a surprising hint of rich cocoa. There's ratatouille, a summery French stew of eggplants, tomatoes, and zucchini. And, of course, pasta alla Norma, which capitalizes on eggplant's meaty texture and affinity for tomatoes.

WHEN TO FIND IT

Eggplant has a fairly short season, two months max, in August and September.

In the Caucasus and Middle East, cooks play up eggplant's slight smokiness, with roasted eggplant dips such as baba ganoush. This complexly flavored dip is incredibly easy to make: Poke a few holes in an eggplant and roast it until it collapses (say an hour at 425 degrees F). Let it cool, scrape out the pulp, and blend it with garlic, lemon, parsley, and a little tahini (just a tablespoon or two will make the dip creamy enough without overwhelming the eggplant).

Eggplants are also delicious grilled. Slice the fat purple eggplants thickly or cut Asian eggplants in half the long way. Brush them with oil and maybe some seasoning, like hot pepper, soy sauce, or ginger and grill until the flesh is creamy. This is absolutely delicious in a sandwich, whether you take it in an Asian direction, such as a vegetarian bánh mì, or a Mediterranean direction, with feta cheese and tomatoes.

Eggplants do have bitter undertones in their flavors, and some people salt them before cooking. (Other people maintain that the bitterness is essential to the eggplant's taste and leave it alone.) You can sprinkle sliced eggplant with coarse salt and leave it in a colander to sit for about a half hour. Then brush off the salt and pat dry to remove most of the juices. Or, using a technique more common in Asian cooking, soak eggplant slices or wedges in cold ice water for fifteen minutes. Dry completely before cooking.

At the market, look for firm, heavy eggplants with a uniform texture. They shouldn't have especially hard or especially soft spots. Their skin should be taut, not wrinkly. Eggplants will keep well for a week or two in the fridge in a plastic bag.

EGGPLANT TOMATO SAUCE

By Elizabeth Millard

Elizabeth Millard farms with her partner, Karla Pankow, at Bossy Acres. They represent the newest generation of farmers: digitally savvy and strategically diversified. They grow more than 50 crops and sell them to CSA members and restaurants, as well as at a handful of farmers markets around the Twin Cities.

Millard says she loves the "nice, smoky, deep flavor" eggplant gives to ordinary tomato sauce. Because you leave the skin on both the eggplant and the tomatoes, it is chunky, hearty, and earthy.

2 pounds tomatoes, quartered 1 pound eggplant, cut into 1" cubes 2 tablespoons cup olive oil 1 teaspoon kosher salt 1 tablespoon mixed dried spices	Preheat oven to 400°F. Mix all ingredients and spread on a roasting sheet. Roast 45 minutes. Transfer everything, including all the juices to a blender or food processor and pulse, but don't liquefy. The sauce will be thick and chunky. *Makes enough for 1 to 2 pounds of pasta.*

✳

Eggplants come in many colors and sizes, from the familiar fleshy
purple-black oblongs to adorable globe shapes in pink, white, green, or purple.

EGGPLANT PARMESAN

By Eric Larsen

Eric Larsen of Stone's Throw Urban Farm learned this dish from an Italian roommate while he was in AmeriCorps and forced—quite happily—to start cooking on his own. "It's the first dish I like to make when the eggplant comes in," he says. Broiling the eggplant instead of frying it not only lightens it up a little bit, but it makes the dish a little sturdier. It also speeds up the process enough to make it a plausible choice for a weeknight.

2 large Italian eggplants, about 2 pounds

1 tablespoon salt, divided

1½ cups flour

2 eggs, beaten

1½ cups dried, unseasoned breadcrumbs or matzo meal

2 teaspoons mixed dried herbs, such as basil, oregano, and marjoram

3 cups flavorful marinara sauce, preferably homemade

2 cups (8 ounces) shredded mozzarella cheese

1 cup (3–4 ounces) freshly grated Parmesan cheese

Slice the eggplant into ½" rounds. Place in a wide colander, toss with 2 teaspoons of the salt, and let stand for at least 20 minutes in the sink. Rinse eggplant thoroughly and pat dry.

Place flour in a sturdy plastic bag with one-third of the eggplant slices; seal and toss until slices are coated evenly with flour. Remove eggplant and repeat with remaining slices of eggplant, adding more flour to the bag if necessary.

Preheat your oven's broiler. In a shallow, wide bowl beat the eggs. Mix the breadcrumbs, herbs, and remaining teaspoon of salt in another shallow bowl. Dip each eggplant slice into the beaten eggs, then into the breadcrumbs to fully coat each side. Arrange the breaded eggplant on a greased baking sheet, or one covered with a sheet of parchment paper.

Broil for 5 minutes until golden brown, flip and broil another 2–3 minutes until golden brown. Remove from baking sheet.

Preheat oven to 375°F. In a small bowl, combine the mozzarella and Parmesan cheeses. In a lightly oiled 9x13" baking dish, spread a cup of marinara sauce over the bottom. Arrange about half the eggplant slices over the top, cover with another cup of sauce and a half the cheese mixture. Repeat and use the remaining sauce and cheese on the final layer.

Bake for 30–40 minutes, until bubbly around the edges and the cheese is slightly browned on top. Let cool 5 minutes and serve.

Serves six to eight.

EGGS

WHILE YOU'RE LOADING up your bag with veggies at the farmers market, don't forget to keep an eye out for other grocery staples, such as eggs. Eggs from the market are fresher and more flavorful than anything you can find in the grocery store.

Believe it or not, eggs used to be a seasonal food. The hens would take a break from laying in the winter when the days were short and then start up again in the early spring. Generally speaking, hens need about fourteen to sixteen hours of daylight as a signal to lay, so eggs would start showing up in laying boxes shortly after the spring equinox.

Today, of course, egg producers provide electric light so that the birds keep laying all winter long. (Yet, we still associate eggs with springtime.) You can, however, sometimes taste the difference between summer eggs and winter eggs. During the warmer months, when the birds have access to plenty of grass and bugs as they peck around outdoors, they will produce eggs with rich, thick, bright orange yolks. During the winter, when they're living entirely on the grain provided by the farmer, the yolks tend to be much paler and thinner.

If you're like most Americans, you keep your eggs in the refrigerator, but you've heard that in Europe and other countries around the world, eggs are stored on the counter. The difference is that eggs produced for sale in this country are almost always washed before sale, and this removes the thin protective coating that prevents bacteria from entering and prolongs the freshness of the egg. Egg producers are also required to refrigerate eggs for sale, and you should also refrigerate eggs you bring home from the market.

Eggs will keep in the refrigerator about five weeks. If you're unsure how old your eggs are, put them in a bowl of water. If they lie flat, they are fresh. If they stand up on end, they are getting old and you should use them up. If they float, they have gone bad and you should discard them. This sounds like a magic trick, but it works because gas builds up between the membrane and the shell as eggs age, causing very old eggs to float.

WHEN TO FIND IT
All year round!

✳
**Believe it or not, eggs used to be a seasonal food. It's thanks
to electric light that hens keep laying all winter long.**

You're unlikely to get old eggs at the market, but you definitely want to ask your
seller when the eggs were laid because, believe it or not, there is such a thing as too
fresh an egg. A freshly laid egg is a thing of absolute beauty when cracked into a
frying pan for breakfast, but it will cause nothing but tears if you try to hard-boil
it. In a fresh egg, the proteins in the white are still tightly bound together. When
you crack it, you'll see that it sits up nice and tall and doesn't spread as much as an
older egg. When you hard-boil it, the white will be custardy, rather than firm. The
membrane of the egg is also thick and stuck tightly to the shell. This makes it almost
impossible to peel a fresh egg. Wait until eggs are at least a week old to hard-boil
them and at least three days old to whip the egg whites. These issues never arise
when you're at the grocery store, because eggs almost always travel at least a week
from commercial producers to grocery shelves.

Some people crow over the virtues of brown or white eggs, but the truth is that
the only thing the color of the shell can tell you is what variety of chicken laid the
egg. Eggs can be snowy white, cream-colored, peach-brown, dark chocolate brown,
and even green or blue. But you won't see any difference after you crack them open.
In addition to colored eggs, you're also far more likely to see unusual eggs at the
farmers market than in the grocery store. Sometimes hens lay eggs that are a little

wrinkly or outsized or tiny or double-yolked. These are all okay to eat even though they look funny.

Market eggs are also more likely to have been produced by a flock with a rooster in it and so might be fertilized. (Remember, hens don't need a rooster around to lay eggs.) Some people believe fertilized eggs have special health benefits, but science doesn't bear this out. Don't worry, however, about finding a developing chick in there: The eggs are kept too cool for any development. Also, all egg producers "candle" their eggs, which means they shine a light through the shell to look for imperfections and signs of development.

While you're buying your eggs, have a conversation with the farmer about his or her flock. Where do they live? Do they get organic feed? Does he or she give the birds antibiotics and if so, is it a matter of course or just when needed? How much time do the birds spend outside? Do they range around the whole farm? Are they on pasture (grass) a significant amount of time? Chickens with access to pasture eat grass and bugs that greatly increase the amount of omega-3 fatty acids in their eggs.

SCRAMBLED EGGS DELUXE

By Sue Zelickson

This rich, creamy scramble, in Zelickson's words, "adds a kick to brunch!" And how.

8 eggs	Beat eggs with sour cream, mustard, salt, pepper, and Worcestershire sauce or salsa. Cut avocado into cubes and sprinkle with a little additional salt. Melt butter in frying pan and add egg mixture, stirring constantly. When almost set, add avocado and fold in carefully. Serve immediately.
½ cup sour cream or cream cheese	
1 teaspoon Dijon mustard	
1 teaspoon salt	
1 teaspoon freshly ground pepper	
¼ teaspoon Worcestershire sauce or 1 tablespoon salsa	
1 avocado	*Serves six.*
1 tablespoon butter	

FENNEL

A WHOLE FENNEL BULB with a two-foot frond waving above it can be an intimidating thing. It can wave jauntily out of the top of your market bag until you get it home and lay it out in its full glory on the counter and wonder what on earth you can do with it.

Answer: lots. Fennel has so much terrific flavor—licorice-y, earthy, and sharp—that it doesn't take much at all to add personality to a dish.

The bulbs can be braised whole or sliced—mint is a natural accompaniment—for a delicious side dish, but most of the time you're going to want to use fennel, in judicious amounts, in other dishes. It brings a wonderful warm note to chicken soup and to beef stew. Sliced and sautéed with apples, fennel goes well with pork.

Fennel can be eaten raw, but its flavor is so intense that it's best in raw dishes when shaved very, very thinly. Shaved fennel with a citrus dressing and some segments of fruit is a classic.

The layers of the fennel bulb can trap dirt, so it's best to swish it in cold water after you slice it. The bulb browns quickly after slicing, too, but a little lemon added to the water will prevent this. The easiest way to slice fennel is on the diagonal: Place it on the cutting board with the base facing you and slice against the grain until you reach the core; then flip it around and slice diagonally again. Discard the core.

The whole fennel plant is edible, but the fat stalks are tough, even when cooked. It's best to discard these (or add them to your vegetable stock) and use the softest, most feathered fronds. These can be chopped and added to soup, tossed with pasta, made into a pesto, or even steeped for tea. To dry fennel fronds, hang the stalks in a dry place with plenty of air circulation. When there is no moisture left at all, remove the crumbly fronds, discard the stalks, and place the dried herb in a clean, dry container.

Most grocery stores sell fennel with the fronds removed, but at the market you're far more likely to find

WHEN TO FIND IT
Fennel is available from late July through early September.

the bulbs and frond intact. Look for fat white bulbs about the size of your fist with fresh, soft, bright green fronds and a relatively fresh-looking cut across the base. Take a sniff, too, and make sure that it smells bright, fresh, and like licorice.

To store, remove the fronds and wrap them separately. They'll be good for about a week in the fridge, while the bulbs will last about two.

Pack-Shot/Shutterstock.com

✳
What on earth do you do with fennel? Slice it thin and dress it with citrus or cook it with apples; chop it and add it to salads, soups, stews, pasta, and pesto.

CABBAGE AND FENNEL SLAW

Courtesy of the Mill City Farmers Market

The Mill City Market is known not just as a place to shop but as a place to watch some of the area's top chefs (and plenty of amateurs too!) demonstrate innovative ways to use the produce and other foods for sale at the market. This is a simple new take on cole slaw.

1 cup corn, cut from one ear
½ bulb fennel, finely chopped
1 tablespoon olive oil
1 teaspoon salt
Freshly ground pepper to taste
¼ cup apple cider vinegar
4 tablespoons honey
½ head cabbage (purple or green), finely chopped

Cook the corn and fennel with the olive oil, salt, and pepper over medium heat until softened.

Stir the honey into the apple cider vinegar until dissolved. Toss this dressing with the cabbage and corn-fennel mixture. Garnish with fennel fronds.

GARLIC AND GARLIC SCAPES

ARLIC IS THE CHAMELEON of the aromatic world: Cook it slowly, on low heat, and it gets rich and sweet. Cook it fast and its flavor gets sharper and spicier (and just a second too long will turn it unpleasantly acrid). Cook it whole or in big slices for a mellower flavor; mince it finely for a big, garlicky ka-pow.

Most of the garlic you find in grocery stores is a "soft-neck" variety. The cloves are clumped together without a central stem. In Minnesota farmers markets, however, you find more of the "hard-neck" varieties. These have a thick, stiff central stalk and tend to have fewer, bigger cloves. Hard-neck varieties like our cold weather better than the soft-necks do.

Garlic aficionados will tell you that the hard-necks have deeper, more complex flavors, but it's likely that what they're experiencing is the difference between commercial varieties raised for yield and ease of shipping and heirloom varieties grown on small farms and raised for flavor. In fact, it's worthwhile to wander the aisles of your local farmers market and take note of the wide variability in garlic types. Some are striped purple; some have thick silvery skins. Some are as big as baseballs. Ask the farmer for the names of the varieties you see (chances are the farmer will give a name reminiscent of Russia or Eastern Europe) and buy a few for a taste test. The range of flavors may surprise you.

The size of garlic bulbs and cloves varies even more. Though this doesn't affect flavor, it does affect your recipes. Many recipes call for "a clove of garlic, minced," which could be as little as a half teaspoon or as much as a tablespoon (some giant cloves are even more). If you're aiming for exact results, it's better to think in volume. One medium clove of garlic is generally agreed to yield one teaspoon when minced.

You should also pay close attention to the preparation called for in your recipe. The smaller you cut your garlic, the sharper the flavor will be. Pushing garlic

WHEN TO FIND IT

Garlic scapes and fresh **garlic** are available in the markets in the spring and early summer. Cured garlic should be easy to find throughout the season.

✳
1. Garlic heads. 2. Garlic scapes.

GARLIC SOUP

This comforting soup shows off garlic's sweet and mellow side. To experience the full range of garlic's contrasts, garnish with the gremolata described below.

4 heads of garlic	Heat the oven to 400 degrees. Slice the top ½" off of each head of garlic. Drizzle evenly with the olive oil and wrap in aluminum foil. Bake 45 minutes or until garlic is very soft.
¼ cup olive oil	
4 tablespoons of flour	
1 quart of lightly flavored vegetable or chicken stock	When the garlic has cooled enough to touch, unwrap and pour as much of the oil left in each packet into a saucepan. Squeeze each garlic clove into the pan. Stir in the flour, mashing well with a fork. Cook about 2 minutes over low heat until it smells lightly toasty, rather than floury. Add the stock and stir well. Bring to a boil and simmer about 15 minutes, covered. Taste, then add salt and pepper.
Salt and pepper to taste	

through a press or (even better) grating it on a microplane will break down all those cell walls and yield the harshest, most garlicky flavor, while mincing it (into pieces about one-sixteenth inch), chopping it (into pieces about one-eighth inch), and slicing it yield progressively mellower flavors.

The most magical way to experience the protean powers of garlic is to roast it: Slice about a half inch off the top of a whole head of garlic, being sure to open the tips of all the cloves. Drizzle a little olive oil over it, wrap it in aluminum foil, and bake at 400 degrees for forty-five minutes. The cloves will be creamy, mellow, rich, and sweet and perfect for spreading on toast.

The polar opposite of that silky sweetness is the sharp bite of gremolata, a garnish that brightens the flavors of stews and roasts. Chop a couple of cloves of garlic. Add a handful of parsley, a sprinkling of coarse salt, and the zest of a lemon and start mincing it all together, right there on the cutting board, until you have a uniform mixture.

PAN-FRIED GARLIC SCAPES

While they are great for punching up pesto and other highly flavored condiments, garlic scapes are also mild enough to eat as a side dish.

2 tablespoons sesame oil	Heat the oil in a wide pan over medium-high heat until it shimmers. Add the scapes and cook until they start to blister, about 4 minutes.
4 cups garlic scapes, cut into 2" pieces	
¼ cup soy sauce or tamari	
1 tablespoon fish sauce	Stir together soy sauce, fish sauce, brown sugar, and red pepper flakes. Add this mixture to the pan, cover, and cook another 4 minutes until the scapes are soft.
1 teaspoon brown sugar	
1 teaspoon red pepper flakes	

You've undoubtedly heard of a thousand ways to make peeling garlic easier. A classic method is to blanche the cloves in boiling water for thirty seconds. This softens the skins, but uses up precious time and energy. Professional chefs whack cloves with the flat of their heavy chef's knives. If you're tall and have good leverage, you can lean the heel of your hand on a clove and press down. But the easiest, safest tool is the bottom of a glass jar or a tin can: Put it on your clove and press down. The papery skin will slip off easily. Trim off the woody end.

To save time when cooking, you can certainly prepare your garlic (or onions or other aromatics) ahead of time and store them in a covered container in the refrigerator, but they will lose some flavor. Whatever you do, don't store chopped garlic in oil. Garlic often harbors botulinum spores that are harmless until they are allowed to breed in an anaerobic (oxygen-free) environment such as oil.

In the spring, you'll occasionally see fresh garlic in the markets with a soft skin rather than a papery one. This is garlic before it has been cured and is juicier and sweeter. It needs to be stored in the fridge and used up fairly quickly.

Keep cured garlic in a cool, dry, dark place, such as a paper bag in a cabinet or in a bamboo steamer (like that used in Asian cooking). If it sprouts, don't eat it! Snip off the tops and sprinkle them on a salad, add to dressings, or cook them up in the flavor base for your soups and stews. Or just go ahead and plant it, because this is how garlic propagates. You can use the green tops and eventually you'll have a whole head of garlic growing in a pot.

Hard-neck varieties grow a green, tubular top called a "scape" that twines and curlicues in the spring. Farmers need to cut these off to force the plant to focus energy on the bulb, but they certainly don't put them to waste. Garlic scapes are one of those springtime treats you almost never see in the grocery store. Look for the tangled bundles of bright green tubes in farmers markets and be sure to grab them when you see them. Sliced into inch-long lengths, they are great in stir-fries, and, blended with oil, salt, grated parmesan, and maybe some nuts, they make a fantastic pesto with a light garlicky flavor.

GREEN BEANS

GREEN BEANS ARE an easy sell at most dinner tables: crunchy, with a fresh, bright flavor (if you don't overcook them), they're a gateway vegetable for veggie skeptics.

Like many vegetables, green beans develop surprising flavors when roasted. About fifteen minutes in a 400-degree oven, tossed with a little olive oil and salt, is enough to turn them brown and tasty. If you want to get fancy, toss them with a fair amount of finely grated parmesan before roasting.

If you don't want to turn on the oven, you can get a nice roasted flavor by browning green beans in a hot skillet. Add just a few tablespoons of water and cover for a couple of minutes to finish cooking them all the way through. Green beans are also a welcome, crunchy addition to most stir-fries.

Fresh young beans are delicious raw. If they aren't young and fresh, blanche them before serving them on a crudité platter for dipping or adding them to a salad.

You may see very skinny green beans in the market. These are a French variety commonly called haricots verts. They cook in a flash and don't have any noticeable seeds in the center. They are delicious tossed with a little butter.

Some people use the term "wax beans" to refer to all beans, whether they are green, yellow, or purple, but others use it exclusively to mean the yellow variety. Yellow beans are far less popular in this part of the country than in other areas and so are harder to find. Some varieties taste just like their green counterparts, while others are earthier in flavor and waxier in texture. They like the company of other earthy flavors, such as mint.

Keep your eye out for bundles of beans that look like they just forgot to stop growing. These are Chinese long beans, sometimes called yard-long beans. They can grow up to 30 inches in length, but are more often found at about half that. They cook and taste much like shorter green beans, but are meatier and a little chewier. They are good roasted or sautéed over high heat before being steamed with a splash of soy sauce and fish sauce.

WHEN TO FIND IT

You may find **green beans** in the market all summer long, but they're at their best in July and August.

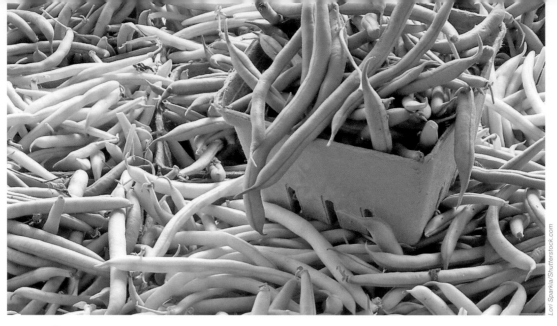

Roast green beans and yellow beans in the oven or brown them in a skillet.

Lori Sparkia/Shutterstock.com

SIMPLE GREEN BEAN SALAD

By Jane Peterson

The Peterson family runs Peterson Turkey Farm and Ferndale Market in Cannon Falls, where they raise turkeys and sell food from other Minnesota growers.

1½ pounds fresh green beans
1 tablespoon finely chopped onion
1 teaspoon salt
¾ teaspoon pepper or to taste
1 tablespoon Dijon mustard
2 tablespoons red wine vinegar
¾ cup olive oil
½ teaspoon fresh lemon juice

Wash and break ends off the beans. Chop or break into 2" pieces. Steam for approximately 6 minutes. Rinse in cold water, drain, and chill. Mix together onion, salt, pepper, mustard, and vinegar. Whisk in the olive oil and lemon juice. Pour dressing over the beans, toss, and refrigerate if serving later. Good made a day ahead.

At the market, look for beans that are firm and snap when you bend them. They should be relatively free of blemishes and uniform in color.

Wash beans well in plenty of cool water, but not until you're ready to use them. Too much moisture will promote rot. They'll keep in a plastic bag in the fridge for one to two weeks (but will taste vastly better the fresher they are). If your beans start to get soft rather than snappy, you can revive them with a half-hour bath in a bowl of ice water. Before cooking, use a paring knife or kitchen scissors to snip off the tips of both ends, since these can be tough, but there's no need to take off more than just the skinniest part of the blossom end and the stem itself.

CHARRED LONG BEANS WITH OLIVES

By Heather Hartman

The Mill City Market opened in 2006, right on the riverfront in downtown Minneapolis. Today the market is a vibrant weekly gathering of people who love good food. Chef Heather Hartman creates recipes and demonstrates cooking techniques at the market, to inspire shoppers to dig into less familiar ingredients, like long beans.

1 bunch, or 1½ pounds long beans (or green beans), cut into 2" pieces

2 teaspoons canola oil

1 teaspoon toasted sesame oil

2 tablespoons minced garlic

2 tablespoons minced ginger

1 Thai chili (or jalapeño), minced

⅓ cup chicken or vegetable stock

2 tablespoons balsamic vinegar or Chinese black vinegar

1 tablespoon soy sauce

¾ cup pitted olives (Moroccan dry-cured or Kalamata olives)

Optional: 4 ounces cooked ground pork or chicken, crumbled

Bring a pot of salted water to a boil. Add the beans and cook 2 minutes. Drain and set aside.

In a large wok or large nonstick skillet, heat oils on high heat. Add the long beans and cook without stirring for 2 minutes. Toss the beans and cook for 1 more minute.

Add the garlic, ginger, and chili pepper, and sauté for 1 minute.

Add the chicken or vegetable broth, vinegar, and soy sauce and cook until almost reduced. Add the olives and cook for 1 more minute. Add the cooked ground pork or chicken if using.

Serve with steamed jasmine rice and a cucumber salad.

Serves four to six.

HERBS

WHILE YOU'RE AT the market picking up the meats and veggies for your main dishes and sides, don't forget to grab a handful—or several—of herbs as well. Fresh herbs are among the best deals at the market, markedly less expensive and much fresher than you'll find them in the grocery store. Herbs, used creatively and in quantities greater than a snip here and there, are also the best way to wake up fresh flavors in your favorite dishes. When you've got a kitchen full of delicious inspiration, you're far more likely to experiment with fresh herbs and use them generously.

Most of the herbs at the market will look pretty familiar. There will be chives, cilantro, dill, lavender, mint, oregano (Mexican and Italian), parsley (curly and flat-leaf), rosemary, and thyme (from lemon to chocolate). There may also be a handful of varieties of basil to try, including Thai purple basil, which has a flavor distinct from the more familiar sweet basil. It's delicious in stir-fries and Asian soups.

But the beauty of shopping at the market is the possibility of discovering herbs you may not have cooked with before. Chervil, for example, is a delicate French parsley that is lovely with fish. Tarragon tastes licorice-y and grassy all at once; it is delicious with rich meats such as lamb, or any dish in which you're using fennel. (Caution: It's easy to go overboard with tarragon.) Marjoram looks a lot like oregano and can be used in many of the same dishes (especially tomato sauces); it's a little more citrusy. Lemon balm (also known as "melissa") is a pungent relative of mint and is terrific for brewing into tea. Shiso, also known as perilla, is a dark purple plant with large leaves and a strong, bitter flavor. A few leaves, sliced thin as a chiffonade, can deepen the flavor of a stir-fry or be sprinkled over grilled meat. Shiso is what gives umeboshi (Japanese pickled plums) their pink color.

The best way to buy herbs at the market is to buy started plants instead of cut herbs. These you can take

WHEN TO FIND IT

Thanks to greenhouses and high tunnels, there's almost always someone selling **herbs**, whether cut or potted, in the market, but the high season is in July, August, and September.

The best way to buy herbs at the market is to buy started plants instead of cut herbs—that way you can have fresh herbs all summer long.

home and stick in a pot with some soil and—voila!—herbs all summer long. If you haven't got the space, or a green enough thumb, plan to use your cut herbs fairly quickly—within three to five days. Most herbs will keep well in the refrigerator, wrapped in a paper towel and placed in a plastic bag. Cilantro, parsley, tarragon, chervil, and shiso will keep even longer if you treat them like cut flowers: Trim a little off the ends and keep them in a glass of water on the counter.

The exception to all this is basil: It will turn brown almost immediately in the refrigerator and will lose its oomph on the counter within a day or two. Plan to use it soon after bringing it home.

Dry your herbs by hanging them in small bunches in a dry, well-ventilated space. (Some people recommend hanging them in the dark, as sunlight will affect the flavor somewhat, but not all of us have that much closet space to spare.) They should be completely dry in a week or two. You can also spread stems of herbs in a single layer, well spread out, on a wire rack set on a cookie sheet, to promote air circulation. Put this out of the way, say, on top of the fridge, for a week or two.

Herbs can be dried in the oven, but it is a delicate business. Again, spread them on a wire rack set on a cookie sheet and set the oven on its lowest setting—"keep warm" if you have it. Check them every minute or so. They will dry quickly.

When herbs are completely dry, strip the leaves from the stems and store them in an air-tight container away from the light. If there is any moisture left at all, the herbs will get moldy.

You can freeze herbs by chopping them finely and packing them into ice cube trays. Cover with water and freeze, then add another thin layer of water and freeze again. This will keep the herbs that floated to the top from being exposed to the air and therefore more susceptible to freezer burn. You can toss a cube or two into winter soups and stews without thawing them out.

1: Fotografiche/Shutterstock.com; 2: Dani Vincek/Shutterstock.com; 3: Freya-photographer/Shutterstock.com; 4: Be. And E. Dudzinscy/Shutterstock.com

✳

1. Dry or freeze fresh thyme. 2. Cut parsley stems and put them in a glass of water.
3. Fresh dill pairs well with cucumbers and potatoes. 4. Use fresh basil as soon as possible.

HERB GARDEN SALAD

By Lenny Russo

This salad from Russo's Saint Paul restaurant, Heartland, is a pure and exuberant expression of the abundance of summer. Taste all the greens you can to find your favorite combination of sweet, bitter, and spicy.

1 cup fresh basil leaves

1 cup fresh chives, bias cut

1 cup fresh chervil leaves

1 cup sweet greens (such as spinach)

1 cup bitter greens (such as dandelion)

1 cup spicy greens (such as watercress)

2 tablespoons grape seed oil

1 tablespoon walnut oil

2 dozen chive blossoms

½ cup walnuts, lightly toasted

1 tablespoon apple cider vinegar

1 teaspoon fine sea salt

½ teaspoon black pepper, freshly ground

Place the herbs and greens in large salad bowl. Sprinkle in the walnuts and chive blossoms. Whisk together the remaining ingredients in a nonreactive mixing bowl. Pour the dressing over the greens. Toss well. Serve immediately.

Serves four to six.

HONEY and MAPLE SYRUP

AMONG THE HEALTHFUL vegetables at most farmers markets, you'll find at least one seller with sweet treats for purchase: local honey or maple syrup. These are well worth the search (and the cash investment), as their flavor cannot be compared with the sugar water that sometimes passes as honey and syrup at the grocery store.

Honey connoisseurs—the ones who know that the flavor can vary from one-note sweetness to complex, caramelly, and bitter—will search the market end to end for single-source honeys. These come from bees that are known to be pollinating only certain fields with a single kind of plant at that particular time. These range from mild-tasting alfalfa and clover honey to deep, dark, rich buckwheat honey.

You may also see other products, such as creamed honey and honeycomb. Creamed honey has been whipped until it is crystallized, but soft and spreadable like butter. Honeycomb is just that: sections of the waxy comb itself, dripping with honey. You eat the whole thing, comb and all, although some people will chew on the waxy comb for a while like gum before spitting it out. Honey sellers also often have beeswax candles and lotions available for sale.

Maple syrup producers are likely to have both grade A and grade B syrup available. Grade A is lighter and milder in flavor, but grade B, which is harder to find in grocery stores, is what maple syrup–lovers and homesick New Englanders crave. Far from an inferior product, it is "grade B" because it is less refined, darker in color, and richer in flavor. It's a good choice if you'll be baking with it, because its flavor is more pronounced, but there's nothing wrong with pouring it over your pancakes.

You might also find birch syrup at some markets, particularly in northern Minnesota where the Finns settled. This is produced in a way similar maple syrup and has a subtle, floral taste.

WHEN TO FIND IT

Honey keeps well and beekeepers—the lucky ones, at least—harvest it all summer long, so there should be some available throughout the market season. **Maple syrup** is easier to find in the spring and early summer, but producers may have some to sell all season long.

✳

1. The flavor of local honey far surpasses what you'll find at the grocery store.
2. The comb in honeycomb is edible, but some chew it like gum and then spit it out.

SPICED HONEY

We can't improve on the work of nature's best honey makers, but we can give a mild honey a little flavor boost. This method also works with 2–3 tablespoons of dried—not fresh—herbs, such as lavender, rosemary, mint, or red pepper flakes.

1 cinnamon stick 10 whole cloves 4 whole star anise 8 whole cardamom pods ½ vanilla pod 1 cup honey	Warm all ingredients gently over low heat and pour into a scrupulously clean jar. Cover and let sit for a week, tilting gently every day to move spices around. After a week, taste it. If you'd like a stronger flavor, leave it for another week. If it's the way you like it, place the jar in a gently simmering pan of water to warm it and strain the honey through a single layer of cheesecloth.

Syrup and honey generally can't be substituted for sugar one to one in baking. You should use recipes specifically developed for their flavors and baking properties (or be prepared to experiment). One delicious way to use honey is to whip it into softened butter. Your pancakes have never been happier. It can also be used, judiciously, in savory recipes. For a decadent dinner, you can coat your chicken in warmed honey before battering and frying or baking it.

Store maple syrup in the refrigerator and honey in the cupboard. If your honey crystallizes, heat it in the microwave for a few seconds or in a gently simmering pot of water.

At the market, take advantage of the seller's samples to find a honey or a syrup you really enjoy. Look for a mild flavor for cooking and baking and a strong flavor, such as buckwheat honey or grade B syrup, for stirring into your tea, drizzling on bread, and just plain savoring. You shouldn't see any evidence of crystallization in the jar and, of course, no floating bits of unidentifiable substances.

MAPLE CARAMEL SAUCE

Maple syrup is delicious on its own, and even more so when you turn it into a creamy sauce. Pour it over ice cream, pancakes, or bowls of fruit.

1 cup maple syrup, preferably grade B ½ cup brown sugar 2 cups heavy cream Pinch of salt	Stir ingredients gently over medium-high heat until sugar dissolves. Bring to a boil, then reduce heat to a low simmer and cook without stirring for 15 minutes, until thickened. To test the consistency, scoop out a small spoonful and let it cool slightly in a bowl. Keeps one to two weeks in the fridge.

Variation: Maple Caramel Candies

Follow recipe above, but continue cooking until mixture reaches 255°F. Line an 8x8" baking pan with parchment paper and pour mixture into pan. Allow to cool in the refrigerator overnight. Slice into 2"-long, ½"-thick candies and wrap individually in parchment paper.

KOHLRABI

KOHLRABI IS AMONG the most baffling vegetables you'll find at the market. The smooth globes with their spindly leaves reaching outward look almost space age, but they're actually an Old World favorite, popular in Germany and Austria. German immigrants brought kohlrabi to Minnesota, where it is especially popular.

The most common advice given to kohlrabi novices who want to know what to do with this strange new vegetable is just to eat it. Kohlrabi is crisp and juicy and tastes like a cross between a cucumber and a broccoli stem. It is particularly good sliced and salted, but there's nothing to stop you from peeling the whole thing and eating it like an apple.

In Europe, however, kohlrabi is usually cooked. It can be grilled or braised—browned over high heat and then steamed with the lid on for a few minutes. A hit of some acid goes well with the sweetness.

Kohlrabi can also be boiled and pureed into a simple soup, finished with mint and cream. In parts of India, kohlrabi is cut into cubes and cooked in a variety of curries. It pairs well with flavors common in that cuisine: coconut milk, coriander, cumin, kaffir lime leaves, and the like.

You'll need to take a good quarter inch of the peel off before eating or cooking your kohlrabi. There are actually two layers to remove: the smooth outer peel and a fibrous interior layer. Slice off the top and bottom of the globe and you'll see a green line running around the inside. Peel off everything from the green line out.

The leaves can be eaten too. They are similar to collard greens and can be sautéed and then steamed. They are often served right along with the flesh of the bulb.

At the market, look for bulbs with the leaves attached (this helps you gauge the freshness of the bulb), but it's certainly not a deal breaker if the grower has removed the leaves. The leaves aren't popular for eating and removing them does make transport easier. Also, look for a clean, fresh cut at the base of the bulb. Larger bulbs

WHEN TO FIND IT

Kohlrabi is at its peak in July and early August.

Laura Stone/Shutterstock.com

✴

Kohlrabi (in purple or green) tastes like a cross between a cucumber and a broccoli stem.

are not necessarily woodier and smaller ones not necessarily sweeter, as each variety matures at a different size, generally three to six inches.

With the leaves removed, the kohlrabi globe can keep up to four weeks in a plastic bag in the fridge. The leaves themselves will keep just one week.

BRAISED KOHLRABI

By Tilia Kitchen

Chef Steven Brown has cooked at just about every restaurant of note in the Twin Cities at some point, but now he has settled down at his own place, Tilia in Minneapolis. He is meticulous, hardworking, and passionate, not just about his work but also about the role good local food plays in the community. And that's why he opened the Linden Hills Farmers Market, down the street from his restaurant, while Tilia was still in its demanding infancy.

At Tilia, this kohlrabi is plated with the Bison in Papaya Marinade (on page 33).

2 pounds kohlrabi, peeled and
   cut into ½" pieces
2 cups water
3 tablespoons red miso paste
3 tablespoons soy sauce
4 thyme stems
1 teaspoon black peppercorns

Combine all ingredients and simmer for 30 minutes or until tender. Allow kohlrabi to cool in liquid.

Serves four to six.

KOHLRABI COCONUT SOUP

This recipe takes kohlrabi out of its Minnesota comfort zone to its subcontinental home.

4 medium kohlrabi, about 2 pounds
1 can unsweetened coconut milk
2½ cups water
1 teaspoon ground coriander
1 teaspoon ground cumin
½ teaspoon turmeric
1 teaspoon ginger
¼ teaspoon cayenne (optional)

Simmer all ingredients for about 20 minutes. Puree until smooth.

Serves four to six.

LAMB and GOAT

L AMB AND GOAT MEAT aren't as easy to find as beef and chicken or even bison, but they are worth seeking out from the growing number of local producers. There are more than 3,000 sheep farms and more than 1,500 goat farms in Minnesota now.

Lamb loves flavors from around the Mediterranean, all the way from Morocco to Greece: fresh and preserved lemons, cinnamon, mint, garlic, cumin, coriander, yogurt, and dill. Use these in marinades, rubs, toppings, and sides and you almost can't go wrong.

Lamb, like beef and pork, has quick cooking and slow-cooking cuts. Lamb chops cook just like pork chops and are great for grilling. All they need is two or three minutes per side over high heat. Rub a little oil and some seasonings on before cooking.

For kebabs, use top round or leg of lamb, cut into two-inch pieces. (Try to buy it already cut, unless you like quality time with your knife.) Marinate the lamb first—yogurt and lemon is great—and then grill the meat for ten to fifteen minutes.

Slower cooking cuts, like a shoulder or leg, whether bone-in or boneless, can be roasted or braised at 350 degrees F, for about 15 minutes a pound until the internal temperature is 145 to 160 degrees F (medium rare to medium well). Take the roast out of oven about 10 degrees early and let it rest for about twenty minutes before carving.

Boost the flavor of a lamb roast by making slits in the flesh and inserting slivers of garlic then rubbing it with oil, salt, and pepper.

Make a lamb stew with your favorite combination of flavors by browning stew meat—just as you would with a beef stew—and then cooking it, covered, with plenty of vegetables and aromatics in a little broth at 325 degrees F for about an hour and a half.

We tend to think of East African or Jamaican cuisine when we think of goat, and then we might remember

WHEN TO FIND IT

Traditionally, young lambs would be slaughtered in March and April, but thanks to the magic of freezers, **lamb** can be found in the market just about any time of year.

that, yes, it's popular in Mexico and India and parts of Italy and, as it turns out, goat is the most widely eaten meat around the world. It's still not mainstream here in Minnesota, but it is getting easier to find, and more producers are showing up at farmers markets.

Most animals have some quick-cooking cuts and some slow-cooking cuts, but pretty much all goat meat is stew meat. So whether you've found bone-in or cubed meat, the easiest way to approach it is the same: Marinate it in something flavorful, at least two hours, preferably overnight, and then cook it in the marinating liquid, covered, at 350 degrees F for two to three hours.

You might go with a marinade of oil, lemon juice, garlic, and plenty of fresh herbs such as rosemary, oregano, and thyme. Or you could go with Jamaican flavors: coconut milk, lots of fresh hot peppers, and Jamaican curry powder.

If you've got a whole leg of goat, you can braise it very, very slowly. After searing it on the stovetop and placing it in a Dutch oven with lots of flavorful vegetables and a little liquid—just like a pot roast—cook it at 300 degrees F for six or more hours, until it is incredibly tender.

At the market, take the time to chat with the grower and learn more about their farming methods and philosophies.

Thaw lamb and goat in the refrigerator. Use thawed and fresh meat within three to five days. Frozen meat will keep in the freezer three to six months or in the deep freeze six to twelve months.

✳
There are more than 1,500 goat farms in Minnesota. Goat is the most widely eaten meat around the world.

LAMB KEBABS

By Kristin Tombers

Clancey's Meats and Fish would be a classic neighborhood butcher shop if it weren't so well-known, respected, and loved that customers from around the Twin Cities seek it out. Owner Kristin Tombers is dedicated to finding the best and most sustainable sources of meat, fish, dairy, and more. What's more, her savvy staff is positively passionate about meat and grilling. No matter what it is you want to grill, they've got tips for you—and if you don't know yet just what it is you're craving, they've got suggestions. The amounts here are all approximate. Kristin likes to cook over a very high heat to get a good char; if you do that, try putting meat and vegetables on separate skewers to better control of cooking times.

1 onion, divided	Grate half the onion on a box grater to use in marinade, reserving all liquid. Cut the other half into wedges and reserve to thread onto skewers.
1–2 pounds cubed lamb meat, such as top round	
¼ cup olive oil	Mix all ingredients together in a medium bowl, squeezing lemons well. Use your hands to blend everything together. Cover and let sit in the refrigerator one hour to overnight.
1–2 lemons, sliced in half, plus more for kebabs	
2 tablespoons dried oregano or ¼ cup fresh	Thread cubes of meat onto skewers (if you use wooden ones, soak them in water for about a half hour beforehand). Alternate with onion wedges and—if you've got some more lemons—small lemon wedges. Push the pieces tightly together on the skewer.
Salt and freshly ground pepper to taste	
5-10 cloves of garlic (or more, to taste), grated, minced, or pressed	Light charcoal grill and wait for coals to ash over or heat gas grill on high for 10 minutes. Grill skewers, turning once, 10–15 minutes, until they reach an internal temperature of 135°F. Remove from grill, tent loosely with foil, and let rest 10 minutes.

GOAT PHÔ

By Stewart Woodman

Stewart Woodman has a reputation in the Twin Cities not only for his cooking chops but also for caring about good food and good cooking—passionately and vocally. He takes his staff on tours of farms, meat-processing plants, and food distributors so that they, and he, can know the whole story of where their ingredients come from. His restaurant, Heidi's Minneapolis—named for his wife and pastry chef, Heidi Woodman—is a landmark on the fine dining scene.

Woodman's goat phô brings together what are by now typically Minnesotan flavors: goat, a staple in the diet of the Somali community, and phô, the beloved Vietnamese soup. Use this rich broth as the base of a simple soup by adding (just before serving) shredded poached goat meat (see below), rice noodles, bean sprouts, basil, sliced chilies, and a squeeze of lime.

1 onion, sliced

1 tablespoon black peppercorns

Canola oil to coat pan

4 star anise

2 cinnamon sticks

2 lemongrass stalks, sliced

1 4" piece of ginger, peeled, sliced

3 Fresno chilies, sliced in half

2 quarts goat stock*

½ cup mushroom soy sauce (or substitute regular soy sauce)

1 bunch cilantro

Sauté onion and peppercorns over high heat in canola oil to achieve lots of caramelization. Add star anise, cinnamon, lemongrass, ginger, and chilies. Sauté for about 5 minutes until soft.

Add goat stock. Bring to a boil and reduce to a simmer. Simmer about 25–30 minutes. Remove from heat, add soy sauce and cilantro. Steep for about 30 minutes.

Strain the phô and cool rapidly.

*To make goat stock, ask your farmers market vendor for goat bones. Roast them in a 450°F oven about 1 hour. Remove to a pot, cover with water, and bring to a boil. Then skim off the scum that floats to the top, reduce heat, and simmer, covered, a good long time, 3-plus hours.

Or make broth using goat meat. Cover pieces of goat with cold water, bring to a boil, and simmer, covered, about 2 hours. Add water as needed.

MELONS

I F LATE SUMMER has a flavor, it is musky, sweet, sticky melon—whether it's chilled and refreshing or sun-warmed and minutes off the vine.

Market melons are likely to be even sweeter and softer than grocery store melons because many growers will harvest their melons at the peak of their ripeness, rather than beforehand, as commercial growers do. This also makes them more fragile and shortens the length of time they can be stored—truly a fleeting treat.

You'll almost certainly see watermelons, honeydew, and cantaloupes at the market, but you might see some unfamiliar melons as well. Keep your eye out for golden-fleshed watermelons, which are less cloying than pink ones, as well as Minnesota midgets (a type of cantaloupe) and tiger-striped melons with crisp white flesh.

If there are Hmong sellers at your market, you will almost certainly see bitter melons, popular in East Asian cooking. Bitter melons are also members of the cucurbit family, but they're different from their sweet cousins. They are long, like fat cucumbers, wrinkly, and pale green. They are not eaten raw, but, rather, are sliced up for stir-fries and stews—beloved for their extraordinarily bitter flavor. (This can be reduced, but not eliminated, by blanching the melon slices in plenty of water before cooking.) To use, slice them open the long way, scoop out the seeds, and slice the halves into half moons or long diagonal strips.

The proper way to identify a ripe melon is one of life's great mysteries, and you're sure to hear conflicting advice. Some people will tell you to rap on it and listen for a hollow sound. Others will tell you to press on the blossom end—it should be slightly soft but not too soft. The best thing to do is trust your nose: A ripe melon will smell like melon. There should be no hard spots and certainly no soft spots on the melon, but don't be put off by some cosmetic scratches or a little discoloration where the melon sat on the dirt.

Beware: Melons go from sweet and musky to overripe and funky seemingly in a matter of minutes. Keep ripe honeydews and cantaloupes in the fridge and plan to use

WHEN TO FIND IT
Melons ripen in August and September and find a sweet spot in late August.

✳

Melons at the farmers market are likely to be sweeter and softer than grocery store melons, because local growers usually harvest them at their peak, rather than beforehand.

them within three to five days. If they're not quite ripe yet, you can keep them on the counter or hasten their ripening in a paper bag with an apple. (Again: Keep a close eye on this process.) Watermelon will keep just fine on the counter, but some people prefer to store it in the fridge because they like the flavor better cold.

Wash the rinds of all melons well, rubbing with a soft cloth, before cutting into them. Even produce from reputable growers can have bacteria on the skin that can be transferred to the flesh as the knife passes through it.

Freeze excess melon in small chunks. When cooler weather comes, you can blitz these in the food processor to make an easy granita that tastes of late summer.

CHILLED MELON SOUP

By Lenny Russo

A cold fruit soup is just the thing for brunch on a summer day, or to start dinner on a hot evening. Lenny Russo serves this at his Saint Paul restaurant, Heartland.

4 quarts coarsely chopped flesh of assorted ripe melons

2 cups sweet white wine such as Riesling or Muscat

1 cup fresh mint, chopped

1 tablespoon ground cinnamon

2 teaspoons ground ginger

1 teaspoon ground nutmeg

1 teaspoon ground allspice

½ cup honey

Purée all ingredients in a blender on high until smooth. Serve chilled, garnished with crème fraiche and raspberries, if desired.

WATERMELON PUNCH

By Sue Zelickson

Local food maven Sue Zelickson notes that this is a great way to use up leftover watermelon—
a concept that's hard to grasp until the summer wanes and the watermelon we once swooned over
seems mundane. If you can't find superfine sugar (also called caster sugar), process regular sugar in
a food processor until fine.

2½ cups watermelon
   hunks, with the rind
   and seeds removed
2 tablespoons fresh lime juice
1 cup fresh lemon juice
¼ cup superfine sugar
2½ cups seltzer water, chilled
Ice

In a blender, pulse the watermelon until smooth. Push it through
a fine-mesh sieve. You should have at least 1¼ cups of
juice. In a pitcher, combine the watermelon, lime and lemon
juices, and the sugar. Whisk until the sugar has dissolved.
Refrigerate until chilled.
Add the chilled seltzer and stir gently. Pour over ice-filled
glasses. Garnish with a slice of watermelon.

Makes about 4½ cups.

MUSHROOMS

SHOWY, FLAVORFUL WILD MUSHROOMS have almost nothing in common with their workhorse cousin, the supermarket button mushroom. The button mushroom is great when you need to bulk up a recipe and it soaks up butter sauces like a pro, but it doesn't bring much to the table in terms of flavor. The mushrooms you can get at the market—whether they are wild or cultivated—are, generally speaking, flavor powerhouses.

In fact, you're unlikely to see plain old button mushrooms at the market. Instead, you might see cultivated oyster mushrooms or shiitakes or those beloved spring-time divas—wild-harvested morels. At this time no one in Minnesota is licensed to harvest and sell other types of wild mushrooms (such as chanterelles, porcini, or chicken of the woods) but that's likely to change as shoppers gain more of an appetite for foraged foods.

As for what kind of mushroom to buy, the best way to decide is to buy what you see and try them all. Morels are nutty and oyster mushrooms are mild. Mix them together in your dish, so that you get a full range of their flavors.

Since mushrooms are packed with water, the trick to cooking them well is to do so quickly, over fairly high heat, and in plenty of fat, before that water has a chance to start coming out. Once the mushrooms start shedding water, you will be boiling, not searing them. The temperature in the pan will drop and you will have a rubbery dish. Give the mushrooms plenty of room, so they don't steam each other, and add any flavoring—garlic, herbs, salt, pepper—after they've had a chance to cook for a minute or two.

If you're going to use mushrooms in a recipe, such as a frittata, pasta dish, or sauce, always cook them first and then add them, so that they don't make your final dish watery.

A classic French preparation of mushrooms is to mince them—whatever sort you have and, again,

WHEN TO FIND IT

There's almost always some kind of mushroom in season, starting with **morels** in early spring through early summer. If there's enough rain, **oyster mushrooms** can be found throughout the season, but especially in the fall.

Don Bendickson/Shutterstock.com

✳

In Minnesota, morels show up in very early spring.

preferably a mixture—finely and then cook them for about five minutes in plenty of fat (olive oil, butter, duck fat), along with shallots and maybe some garlic. The paste you get is called duxelles and is a base flavoring for so many tasty dishes. Stir it into soup, stuff it inside a roast, spread it on crunchy toast to make a fancy appetizer—or just breakfast.

You may have heard that you should not wash mushrooms because they will soak up too much water, but this isn't true. (Mushrooms are mostly water, remember?) But you do want your mushrooms to be completely dry before you cook them, so if you rinse them off, pat them dry. The best way to wash mushrooms is the most labor intensive: one by one with a dry kitchen towel, gently but firmly brushing off any dirt. If your mushrooms have open gills, trim these out with a knife. Remove shiitake stems, but most other mushroom stems are fine to eat. Most important, do not wash or cut your mushrooms until you are ready to use them.

A little dirt on the mushrooms in the market is fine, but they shouldn't look bruised or slimy at all. They should smell like fresh dirt or the forest floor and be plump, not limp.

If you find dried mushrooms at your market, you can rehydrate them by soaking them in hot water for about fifteen minutes and then use them in soups, stews, and sauces. Dried mushrooms will have a more intense flavor than fresh mushrooms.

Now, you might be a little wary of buying wild mushrooms from an unknown source—especially if you're not confident in your own abilities to differentiate the poisonous mushrooms from the tasty ones. (There is no mistaking a morel, however, with its elongated webbed cap.) You should ask the seller at the market about his or her experience and training. In Minnesota, foragers must have a license from the Minnesota Department of Agriculture to sell wild mushrooms harvested anywhere other than on their own land. And, even if they do harvest on their own land, they need documentation that they have taken a wild mushroom identification course.

Some market sellers of cultivated mushrooms have also started packaging mushroom kits (usually oyster mushrooms). Often the economics don't quite add up—for the price, you could buy more mushrooms than your kit will yield—but the entertainment value is quite high.

Plan to use up your mushrooms quickly. Keep them in a paper bag in the fridge for just a couple of days. A plastic bag will trap moisture and speed rot. Mushrooms don't freeze well. If you freeze them raw, the ice crystals will destroy their cell structure and they'll turn to mush. You can freeze duxelles fairly well. If you have more mushrooms than you can use, you can pickle them.

GRILLED MUSHROOM and ROASTED GARLIC PIZZA

By Jeremy McAdams

Jeremy McAdams cultivates shiitake, oyster, and nameko mushrooms in logs at Cherry Tree House Mushrooms in Maplewood. He created this wildly flavorful pizza recipe and demoed it at the Mill City Farmers Market.

3–4 ounces fresh oyster mushrooms, chopped	1–1½ cups cherry tomatoes
½ roll of pizza dough	Salt and pepper to taste
2 tablespoons flour	3–5 ounces mozzarella cheese
About ¼ cup olive oil	1–2 ounces Parmesan or Friesago cheese
2 small to medium heads of garlic	

Thaw pizza dough in refrigerator. A few hours before cooking, bring to room temperature on floured surface until doubled in size. Roll out dough until thin using rolling pin or stretching by hand. Use flour as needed to keep dough from sticking to surface or rolling pin. Place on well-floured (and movable) chopping block.

Preheat oven to 400°F. Peel away outer layers of garlic heads, but without removing skin on individual cloves. Then trim off one-quarter to one-half of the top of the bulb with a knife, exposing the tops of the cloves. Put garlic heads in baking pan, then drizzle with 1 to 2 teaspoons of olive oil. Cover the heads with aluminum foil and cook in the oven until garlic is soft, about 30 minutes.

You can roast the tomatoes at the same time that you roast the garlic. Wash the tomatoes, then slice in half. Place tomato halves in baking pan, cut side up, and drizzle with olive oil. Sprinkle with a little salt and pepper and cook until soft and browned.

Prepare grill. Grate or crumble cheeses.

Clean mushrooms by running under cool water and rubbing away soil with fingers or by soaking in water, then place on towel to dry. Trim away less fleshy stems and save for soup stock. Slice larger caps into smaller pieces. Heat 1 to 2 tablespoons of olive oil on medium-high heat, and cook mushroom caps until soft and slightly browned, about 5 minutes. If mushrooms look dry, add more oil to pan. Set aside.

Place pizza crust on hot grill until the crust is firmed up a bit, about 3 minutes. Remove the crust from the grill. Spread grilled side with roasted garlic, tomatoes, and any oil from their roasting, then top with mushrooms and cheeses. Place pizza back on grill and cook until the bottom is firm and cheese has melted. Remove from grill, then slice and serve immediately.

SPINACH WITH MUSHROOMS

By Sue Zolickson

Sue Zelickson says that this lighter, simpler dish is inspired by the creamed mushrooms served at fine steakhouses around the country.

1 tablespoon of olive oil	Heat olive oil in a large sauté pan over medium-high heat until shimmering. Add mushrooms and cook until starting to brown, about 5 minutes. Work in batches, if necessary, to avoid crowding the mushrooms. Stir in garlic for the last minute of cooking. Remove mushrooms from pan and set aside.
1 pound of mixed fresh mushrooms, coarsely chopped	
1 clove garlic, minced	
1 large bunch fresh spinach, coarsely chopped	Add spinach to hot pan and turn it over in the hot pan with tongs or a large spatula until it wilts. Reduce heat and cook until it is tender, about 5 minutes. Remove pan briefly from heat and tilt it into the sink to drain of any excess liquid.
¼ cup sour cream	
Salt and pepper, to taste	Stir mushrooms and sour cream into spinach. Add salt and pepper to taste.
	Serves six.

ONIONS, LEEKS, and SHALLOTS

WHEN YOU'RE NOT quite sure what you're going to cook, it never hurts to peel and chop an onion, put it in a pan with some oil or butter, and start cooking it down while you ponder your next steps. The cooked onion is the foundation for any number of dishes.

Add carrots and celery and you have a French mirepoix. Add bell peppers and celery and you have the Holy Trinity of Cajun cuisine. With garlic and celery, it's an Italian soffrito. And with garlic and tomatoes, it's a Spanish sofrito. All of these bases take you most of the way toward a soup, stew, or sauce.

Onions are like the folks working tech on a theater production: They're essential to the success of the show (and the dish), but if things go well, you never notice them. Onions, however, deserve to take center stage every once in a while. They're inexpensive, complexly flavored, and versatile. If you start your onions in cold oil and keep the heat low, they soften and become translucent, getting sweeter and sweeter as you cook them. Once they have completely broken down, they will turn golden and sticky, then deepen in color. These, cooked with patience and vigilance, are caramelized onions. Add herbs and broth and cook some more and you've got French onion soup.

If you heat the oil before you add the onions, they start to brown quickly. They grow more sharply flavored instead of sweeter. This gives them a meaty flavor that goes great with potatoes of all sorts. And if you use quite a bit of oil, say an inch or two in the bottom of a heavy pan, and heat it to 375 degrees before adding very, very thinly sliced onions, after about ten minutes of frying you get a decadent, crunchy onion topping.

Many people enjoy a sliced raw onion on a salad or on a burger, but others find the sharp flavor intrusive and unpleasant. Soaking thinly sliced onions in vinegar for fifteen or twenty minutes will get rid of the strong flavors (and soften the onions). Drain well, discarding the vinegar.

WHEN TO FIND IT

Fresh onions are available in spring, **dried onions** later in the summer and fall. **Spring onions** and **leeks** are available for most of the market season.

✳

Yellow onions are for all-purpose cooking. Red onions are milder and better for using raw.

Your shopping list may just say "onions," but there are a few more choices to make once you get to the market. In the spring and early summer, fresh onions will be available. These were planted in the winter and grew in the cold ground as soon as it thawed, making them a little sweeter. They're harvested while the tops are still green and often sold with the tops attached. (You can snip the tops off and use them like scallions.) Fresh onions are juicer than dried onions and need to be stored in the fridge. If you find ones with small bulbs, snap them up and put them on the grill.

Dried onions are harvested after the green tops have died back and are then cured. Yellow onions are your all-purpose cooking onions, while white and red ones are milder and better for raw uses. When you buy dried onions, the papery skin should still be tight and the onion should feel heavy in your hand. Definitely don't buy onions that have started to sprout or have powdery mold on the surface.

They will keep for a month or more, if stored in a cool, dry, dark space. A paper bag in a cabinet, away from heating ducts, works well. If you keep your onions on the counter, they will most likely start to sprout. If this happens, you might as well let them grow for a while, as is, then snip off the green tops as they grow and use them like spring onions. Discard the bulbs, which will get soft and flavorless.

When you cut into an onion, the knife breaks the cell walls, releasing sulfurous compounds into the air, and suddenly you look like you've been watching *Sophie's Choice*. The best way to cut down on tears is to soak the onions in a bowl of icy cold water for a half hour. This reduces the volatility of the sulfur and—bonus!—will soften the peel so it comes off more easily. If you don't have time to soak, rinse your knife in cool water before you start cutting and keep rinsing it or wiping it down with a wet cloth as you work.

Scallions, also called spring onions or green onions, are young onions that have been grown close together and harvested before bulbs formed. These will be plentiful in the markets in the spring, because they can be sown early and grow quickly, but they are generally available throughout the market season.

1: Prill/Shutterstock.com; 2: Chamille White/Shutterstock.com; 3: Digidreamgrafix/Shutterstock.com; 4: Successo/Shutterstock.com

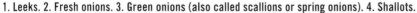

1. Leeks. 2. Fresh onions. 3. Green onions (also called scallions or spring onions). 4. Shallots.

Shallots are not just small onions. They are their own species and have their own distinct flavor, sweeter and less sulfurous than onions. They grow in heads like garlic, with detachable cloves that are each flat on one side. These should also be stored in a dark, cool place. A bamboo steamer, the kind used in Asian cooking, is a great choice and keeps them close at hand on the counter. You can use shallots in just about any recipe that calls for onions. Because they are more expensive, you may want to deepen the flavor of your onions by mixing in just one or two shallots.

Leeks are the nonbulbing cousins on the onion family tree. They have fat, white stalks and tough fans of greens. Look for leeks with substantial white stalks, because

SWEET VIDALIA ONION PIE

By Carrie Boyd

As manager of the Onamia Area Farmers Market, Carrie Boyd says she is often asked, "How do you cook that?" or "What in the world do you do with that?!" This quiche-like pie is one answer, when you're looking for a recipe that makes onions the stars of the show.

1½ cup crushed buttery
    round crackers
⅓ cup plus 2 tablespoons
    butter, divided
2 cups sliced sweet onions
2 eggs
¾ cup half and half
¾ teaspoon salt
⅛ teaspoon ground white pepper
¼ cup shredded sharp
    cheddar cheese

Preheat oven to 350 degrees.

Melt ⅓ cup butter and mix with crushed crackers. Press mixture firmly into a 9" pie pan. Melt remaining 2 tablespoons butter in a skillet on medium heat; cook onions until tender and translucent (don't brown). Spread onions into crust. Whisk together eggs, half and half, salt, and pepper. Pour mixture over onions and sprinkle the top with cheese. Bake for 30 minutes until the center is set. Let stand for 10 minutes before cutting.

Serves six.

QUICK RED ONION RELISH

You'll never put raw onions on your burger again. This quick-and-easy relish is also great on tacos and chili.

1 large red onion
½ cup red wine vinegar
1½ teaspoons kosher salt
1 tablespoon brown sugar
1 tablespoon whole cumin seeds
1 tablespoon whole coriander seeds

Slice onions into paper-thin half moons. Stir salt and sugar into vinegar until dissolved. Mix all ingredients together and let sit for one hour. This will keep in the refrigerator for about a week.

Makes 2 cups.

this is the part you eat. (The greens are great for making vegetable stock.) Because farmers keep those stalks white by heaping dirt on the plants as they grow, leeks tend to be full of grit. There are two good ways to wash out the grit: Slice the white part into fat rounds and swish around in plenty of cold water, letting the grit fall to the bottom, or slice the leeks from end to end the long way, keeping the root intact as a handle, and run it under cold water, separating the layers. Nobody loves leeks more than the Scots, who serve them as an easy side dish: Melt butter in a large pan, add fat slices of leeks, turn the heat down, cover and cook about twenty minutes until the leeks are soft, then add salt and pepper as you like.

STUFFED ONIONS

An alternative to classic American stuffed peppers, stuffed onions are popular in the Middle East. While white rice will certainly work in this dish, farro (a chewy, meaty, Italian grain) or brown rice makes it more hearty and flavorful.

1 cup semipearled farro or brown rice

4 large onions

2 tablespoons olive oil

2 medium cloves garlic, chopped

1 cup chopped parsley

1 cup crumbled feta

1 cup chicken stock, vegetable stock,
   white wine, or water

Cook the farro or brown rice in boiling, salted water until tender. Farro will take about 30 minutes, brown rice about 40. Drain and reserve.

Heat the oven to 375 degrees. Lightly grease an 8x8" baking dish (or one of similar size) with olive oil. Put a medium pot of water on to boil.

Trim the root and top ends from the onions and remove the peels. Slice each onion lengthwise halfway through. You should be able remove each layer like a jacket. Keep the three or four outermost layers of each onion for stuffing, and reserve the inner layers.

Boil the outer onion layers for about 5 minutes, until just soft. Set aside.

Chop the inner layers. Heat the olive oil in a wide pan over medium heat and add the chopped onions and salt. Cook until lightly golden, about 8 minutes. Add the garlic and cook until fragrant, about 1 minute.

Mix onion mixture, cooked farro or rice, feta, and parsley taste and adjust seasoning.

Spoon about a quarter cup of filling into each onion layer and roll fairly tightly. Place these close together in the prepared dish and pour the liquid over the tops. Bake, uncovered, about 45 minutes.

Serves four.

PEAS

MOST PEOPLE HAVE one of two childhood memories of peas. Either they remember mushy, starchy, gray blobs staring tauntingly back at them from the plate, or they remember warm summer days with a bowl of fresh-picked peas in their laps, happily shucking and popping candy sweet peas into their mouths at the same time.

Oh, if only we had a time machine so we could go back and share the latter kids' peas with the former. We as a country might have an entirely different relationship with the iconic and often-hated vegetable.

The difference between the gray blobs and the bright green candy is twofold: The mushy peas are older and their sugar molecules have all been converted to starch. And they have had the last bit of life cooked right out of them.

As soon as a peapod is picked off the vine, it starts to get starchy. Within just a day or two, it is no longer the irresistible sweet thing it once was. For that reason—and because they are labor- and land-intensive—they are a rare find in the farmers market. If you do happen to see them—called either "English peas" or "shell peas"—screech to a halt and run over to investigate. Pop open one shell: Is the pea bright green and sweet? If so, buy up as much as you can and block off the afternoon to sit on the porch in the sunshine shelling peas. And, really, you'll want to buy more than you think: Figure on a half-pound of peas in their shells per diner.

Peas this fresh barely need any cooking. (In fact, if you couldn't buy as many as you wanted, you can sprinkle them raw on whatever salad you're having for dinner that night.) You can give them a quick dunk—just a minute or two—in salted, boiling water. Or, even better, swirl them in a warm pan of melted butter with a pinch of fresh mint.

Peas with pasta and prosciutto or pancetta or your cured meat of choice is a classic Italian dish. All you need is a little olive oil and a little parmesan to hold it

WHEN TO FIND IT

Peas are in the market in June and July, and then they are gone until next year. They don't like the hot weather.

✳
Shelled peas this fresh barely need cooking: swirl them in melted butter with a few leaves of fresh mint.

RISI E BISI

Rice and peas—a simple risotto with a simple name and a comforting texture. This is traditionally one of the first solid foods babies eat in some parts of Italy. This version is packed with as many fresh peas as you can get.

5 cups no-sodium chicken or
    vegetable broth, or water
2 tablespoons olive oil
2 medium shallots, sliced
1 cup Arborio or Carnaroli rice
2–3 cups fresh peas
    (frozen will work too)
½ cup freshly grated
    Parmesan or Asiago cheese
1–2 tablespoons butter
Salt and pepper to taste

Bring stock or water to a low simmer on the stove and keep it there. In a wide-bottomed pan over medium heat, cook the shallots in the olive oil until they are quite soft, but not browned.

Increase the heat to medium-high and add the rice. Cook, stirring, for about 3 minutes. Add a cup of hot broth and cook, stirring often, until most of the liquid has been absorbed. Repeat until the rice is al dente and won't absorb any more liquid. Add another splash of liquid and stir vigorously for about 30 seconds to develop the starchy sauce. Stir in peas, Parmesan, and butter. Taste and add salt and pepper.

together and maybe a squirt of lemon. Italian children are also practically weaned on a thin, comforting risotto called "risi e bisi"—rice and peas. The French braise their peas with lettuce. Just heat some olive oil over medium high, add small heads of butter leaf lettuce, sliced in half. When they're beginning to brown, add a splash of stock and some peas. Put the lid on, turn the heat down, wait a couple of minutes, season with salt and pepper and—voila!—summer comfort food. If you are simply drowning in fresh peas, a minty cold pureed soup with yogurt is also lovely on a hot day, but most of us should be so lucky.

In the market, you're more likely to see two types of peas that are not for shelling: snow peas and sugar snap peas. Both of these can be eaten shell and all.

Snow peas are the flat ones with the little bumps peeking through. These keep well and have a less pronounced "pea" flavor. To prep them, all you need to do is wash them and snip off any stem that may still be attached. Some people will toss snow peas raw in a salad, but they're really best when cooked. They like a quick trip in a hot pan; that's why they're a classic ingredient in stir-fries. If you cook them too long, they will turn gray, mushy, and stringy (and perhaps bring back some bad childhood memories).

Sugar snap peas are the ones in the plump edible pods—the ones with the pod walls that are often as thick as the peas themselves and just as tasty. These usually have strings that need to be removed. The easiest way is to put your knife against the convex side of the blossom end and simultaneously snip off the end and pull the string off the inside of the concave side. When you get to the stem end, keep going and take the string off the convex side. (Sound complicated? It needn't be. Spend a few contemplative minutes stringing peas and you will undoubtedly develop your own fine system.)

Sugar snap peas are so delicious raw that you may never even have time to wonder how to serve them, beyond popping them in your mouth. But if you're looking for ideas, they make a great addition to salads and can even make a nice salad themselves, when sliced into bite-sized pieces and tossed with a sweet, citrusy dressing. You can use them in place of English peas in the classic braised lettuce dish above, but they'll need to cook longer, so start them right in the hot pan with the lettuce.

In early June, you'll almost definitely see pea shoots at the market. These are the tender young leaves and stems of the pea plant, which farmers snip off to encourage the plant to keep growing and branching. You'll see them in tangled bundles, usually the first green things in the market. The youngest pea shoots are so tender they can be used just as they are, in salads or as a little salad on their own. Others have, frankly, gotten a little unpleasantly tough. The best way to tell is with your teeth: You'll know when you're picking strings out of your teeth. If your bundle of pea shoots—or, more often, the base of your bundle—is too tough to eat raw, you can chop them and braise them (if they're too tough to eat, they're probably too tough to stir-fry). Or you can boil them for a few minutes and puree them with olive oil, garlic, salt, and lemon juice to make a nice pesto sauce for pasta.

To find the best peas and pea shoots at the market, ask when they were picked, and then ask for a little taste. They should taste springy and sweet. The pods should not look bruised or dried out, and they should be a nice, bright shade of green. Shell peas should be eaten right away, but snap peas and snow peas will keep for about a week in the fridge in a plastic bag. If your snow peas get a little floppy, dunk them in cold water for about a half hour to refresh them.

Shell peas—should you ever be blessed with a surfeit—freeze well as is. Just put them in a plastic bag with most of the air squeezed out and toss them in the freezer. If you really, truly must freeze snow peas or sugar snap peas, be sure to blanche them beforehand, but their texture and flavor won't be the same.

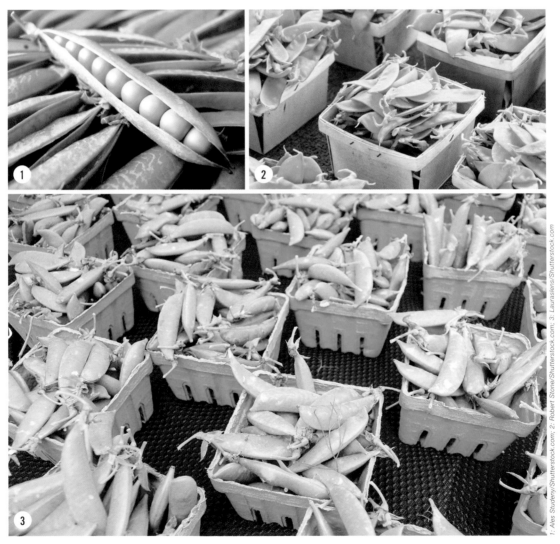

✸
1. Shell peas. 2. Snow peas. 3. Sugar snap peas.

SPRING PEA DIP

By Carrie Boyd

Carrie Boyd, who manages the Onamia Area Farmers Market, serves this springy dip with vegetables such as cucumber strips, yellow and red pepper strips, and baby carrots or pita chips.

1 pound fresh peas in the pod
¼ cup loosely packed fresh
   mint leaves, chopped
¼ teaspoon salt
¼ teaspoon pepper
⅓ cup ricotta cheese
2 tablespoons freshly grated
   Parmesan cheese

Shell the peas. Heat an inch of water to boiling over high heat. Add the peas and bring back to a boil. Reduce heat to medium. Cover and cook 3 minutes or until peas are tender. Drain and rinse under cold water. In a food processor, puree the peas with the mint, salt, and pepper. Place in bowl; stir in ricotta and Parmesan.

PEPPERS

ALL PEPPERS START out green and can be picked at that point. As they mature, they get sweeter and turn yellow, red, purple, or even a chocolate brown. This explains why growers ask a premium for these colored peppers over the green ones: They've been taking up valuable farm real estate for an extra month or more. Some will claim that there is absolutely no difference in flavor between a green pepper and a red pepper, but I challenge you to try a blind taste test of two vine-ripened peppers. One will be more complex and sweeter, and that will always be the red one.

When you're cooking with sweet peppers, the final dish is so much nicer when you peel them. When you've discarded the indigestible peel (this is what gives a lot of people tummy trouble), you're left with the silky smooth meat of the pepper.

Peeling is an extra step, of course, but it's easy. Roast the peppers in a 500-degree oven for fifteen minutes until blistered on every side. You can speed things along by sticking them under the broiler, on high, instead. Some people will hold the peppers with tongs over a gas burner or put them on a hot grill. The whole point is to make the skin puff and brown—or even burn. Put your blistered peppers, while still hot, in a plastic bag or a bowl with a lid and leave them there until they have cooled enough to handle. The skin should come right off in your hands. Reserve the juices while you peel them. This is often a nice addition to whatever you're doing with the peppers and can be handy for storing them.

Roasted peeled peppers are tasty as is, especially on sandwiches and pizzas, but they can also be the base of stews or silky pureed soups. The exception to this rule is in a stir-fry where you generally want tender-crisp veggies, not silky smooth ones, so it's best not to peel peppers before using them in a stir-fry.

There are dozens of varieties of hot peppers, from the mild poblano to the moderately hot jalapeño and serrano to the searing habañero. All of these start out

WHEN TO FIND IT

Peppers arrive at the height of the summer vegetable explosion, in late June, July, and August.

118

Kevin M. Kerfoot/Shutterstock.com

✳

**As a pepper matures, its color changes and its flavor deepens. This is true for
both sweet bell peppers and hot peppers such as jalapeños, serranos, and habañeros.**

green and get hotter as they mature and turn red (or orange, in the case of the
habañero, which is rarely picked green).

The thing about hot peppers is you never know exactly how hot they're going
to be. Maturity is one factor, but so is the weather. (Hot and dry weather makes hot
peppers hotter.) And there's some randomness involved too: The heat of a particular
pepper will vary not just from grower to grower but also from plant to plant. When
cooking with peppers, it's best to start with the minimum and add heat as you're
going along.

Most of a pepper's heat is in the ribs, so you can control the zing in your recipe
by cutting these out (or leaving them in). Handle hot peppers with caution. (There's

a reason pepper spray is called "pepper spray": It's concentrated capsicum, just like someone is shooting habañeros in your face.) Some people wear gloves when handling hot peppers. Others scrub their hands clean. Be sure to wash your knives and cutting boards well when you're done, and never, ever touch your face or eyes while working with the peppers.

Roasting hot peppers—although you'll never be able to peel them as cleanly and easily as sweet peppers, and it's not really worth trying—before using them in your recipe adds a different flavor note that's particularly nice in chili.

At the market, look for smooth, heavy peppers with a deep, uniform color. Peppers will keep in a plastic bag in the fridge for up to two weeks. To dry hot peppers, tie them in small bunches and hang them somewhere where they won't get too much light but will get plenty of air circulation. Or, if they are small, spread them in a single layer on a cooling rack and set it out of the way. When they have shed all of their moisture, you can store them in an airtight container (or leave them hanging up), but if there is any moisture left at all, they will grow mold.

You can also dry peppers in the oven. Cut them in half the long way and scrape out the seeds and ribs. Put the pepper halves and seeds separately on a cookie sheet in the oven at its lowest possible heat (lower than 200 degrees F, if you can). The seeds and ribs will dry faster than the peppers themselves; give them a little stir every once in a while. Again, be sure all the moisture is gone before storing them.

PIPERADE

Piperade is a dish with roots in Basque and French cuisine. It's an easy, satisfying, veggie-filled summer dinner.

2 bell peppers
1 onion, very thinly sliced
4 cloves garlic
1 tablespoon smoked paprika
2 tablespoons olive oil
16 ounces chopped
  tomatoes, canned or fresh
Salt and pepper to taste
4–6 eggs

Heat broiler. Place peppers directly under it, turning to blister them on each side. Place them in a glass bowl and put a plate on top to trap the steam. When cool enough to handle, remove peel and stem and slice peppers into strips.

Cook onions, garlic, and paprika in olive oil over medium heat until soft, about 10 minutes. Add tomatoes and simmer, with the lid on, about 30 minutes. Remove lid and cook uncovered, stirring frequently, to thicken. Taste and add salt and pepper.

Beat together eggs and scramble them in a separate, nonstick pan. You want soft curds, so use medium-low heat and stir almost constantly. Stop just before the eggs are fully cooked. Stir eggs into pepper mixture. Serve immediately.

Serves four to six.

HOT PEPPER VINEGAR

In parts of the South, hot pepper vinegar is an absolutely essential accompaniment to cooked greens. You can also drop a little into soup or onto cooked beans. Any kind of hot pepper will do: shisitos, jalapeños, habañeros, serranos—a mix of colors is especially pretty.

2 cups white vinegar

1 cup assorted
    hot peppers

1 teaspoon whole
    peppercorns

2 whole garlic cloves

Slice peppers in half the long way. To make milder pepper, scoop out the seeds and ribs; for hotter vinegar, leave them in. Place peppers in a clean glass jar with peppercorns and garlic cloves. Bring vinegar to a boil and pour it into the jar. Let it steep for about a week. When it reaches the level of heat you want, strain out the peppers or it will continue to get hotter. Store in the refrigerator.

PLUMS

FRESH, LOCAL STONE FRUIT from Minnesota? Absolutely. As long as you like plums. (There have been a few peach and apricot varieties developed for Minnesota's growing zone, but these are not in commercial production.)

There are a handful of varieties of plums grown here in Minnesota, most of which are bred to be quite sweet and are delicious eaten just as is. They range from the yellow-fleshed La Crescent and Underwoods, early varieties, to the pink, ultra-sweet Tokas (also known as Bubblegums), and deep, deep, deep purple Mount Royal and Black Ice plums.

Plums are delicious in cobblers, of course, but there is so much more they can do in the kitchen. Grill them, cut side down and brushed with a little butter. Roast them with a little sugar and a little butter (fifteen minutes at 400 degrees F should do it). Poach them (pitted) in red wine. Puree them into a cold dessert soup.

Plums are high in pectin, so they are a good choice for easy preserves. Wash, slice, pit, and quarter the plums and cook with an equal weight of sugar. Scrape the seeds from a vanilla pod and add that, too, for a truly decadent flavor. (If you want to drive yourself crazy, but get "jam" rather than "preserves" as your end product, then go ahead and peel your plums.) Cook until the liquid sets up as a gel when you scoop it out with an ice-cold spoon or until it reaches 220 degrees F. You can make jam in small quantities in a wide-bottom pan on the stovetop. It will reach the gelling point quickly and have a fresher, less "cooked" flavor.

You can also preserve your plums in brandy or your tipple of choice. Washed, pitted, and quartered, they go into a jar with a couple of tablespoons of sugar, maybe a cinnamon stick, maybe a vanilla pod, and enough brandy to cover. The jar goes in the refrigerator and in a few weeks—or months—you have brandied plums to put on your ice cream and plum-flavored brandy to drink.

At the market, look for smooth, relatively firm plums with a little bit of a white, powdery bloom on

WHEN TO FIND IT

The first **plums** start ripening in early August and the last ones come in September.

Photo credit: Robert Stone/Shutterstock.com

✳
Plums you might find at a Minnesota market range from the yellow-fleshed La Crescent and Underwoods to the pink Tokas and the deep, deep purple Mount Royal and Black Ice.

them. Look at the stem ends for signs of rot and give them a good sniff: They should smell sweet and fruity, but not overripe or fermented.

The window of time between hard and sour and inedible mush is small for plums. For that reason, it is best to buy them when they are still rather firm—unless you plan to eat them on the spot—and ripen them on the counter in a paper bag. Ripe plums can and should go into the fridge to slow the ripening process, but their texture and flavor will change.

Plums freeze well. Pit them first (a cherry pitter works remarkably well on the small ones) and pack them into plastic bags with as much air squeezed out as possible. You also might want to stir a little sugar in with the plums before freezing—instant pie filling.

GRILLED RIBS WITH PLUM SAUCE

By Carrie Boyd

Plums and pork are a match made in fruity, porky heaven. Carrie Boyd, manager of the Onamia Area Farmers Market, makes this salty-tangy-sweet sauce to bring out the best in her favorite ribs.

6 pounds pork spare ribs
¾ cup soy sauce
¾ cup plum sauce
¾ cup honey
3 minced garlic cloves

Cut ribs into serving-sized pieces. Place bone side down on a rack in a shallow roasting pan. Cover and bake at 350 degrees for 1 hour until ribs are tender; drain. Combine remaining ingredients and brush over ribs. Grill over medium heat for 30 minutes, while continuing to brush with sauce. (You can continue to cook in oven on a rack in a shallow roasting pan uncovered instead of grilling.)

Serves six to ten.

PLUM CATSUP

By Lenny Russo

Once you've assembled the spices, this silky complex sauce, created by Lenny Russo of Heartland restaurant, comes together extraordinarily easily. This will transform your next burger.

9 cups ripe red or purple plums, stoned

1½ cups light brown sugar, packed

1 cup apple cider vinegar

½ cup port wine

½ cup dry red wine

2 whole garlic cloves, chopped

2 shallots, chopped

2 cinnamon sticks

1 teaspoon fresh ginger, grated

½ teaspoon ground allspice

½ teaspoon ground mace

½ teaspoon ground nutmeg

¼ teaspoon ground cloves

2 teaspoons fine sea salt

1 teaspoon cayenne pepper

1 bay leaf

Place the plums in a nonreactive saucepan with the sugar, vinegar, and wine. Bring the pot to a simmer over medium-low heat. Add the shallots and garlic. Simmer for 5 minutes and add the remaining ingredients. Continue to simmer until the sauce begins to thicken (about 20 to 25 minutes). Remove the bay leaf and cinnamon sticks. Transfer the catsup to a blender or food processor and purée until smooth. Allow the catsup to cool in the refrigerator. The natural pectin will thicken the sauce. The catsup may be served warm, cold, or at room temperature.

Makes about 3 pints.

Foodiepics/Shutterstock.com

✷

For a different take on plums, grill or roast them and serve with ice cream.

PORK

I F YOU ARE NOT eating Midwestern heritage pork, you are missing out. So says chef Lenny Russo, who has been shouting from the rooftops about local and sustainable food since long before people were listening.

Russo serves pork in all sorts of ways at his restaurant, Heartland, in Saint Paul, from chops and tenderloins to house-made sausages and chicharrones (fried pork skin).

"We're sitting in pork central here," he says. "It's really remarkable, the number of people raising quality pigs. And pork is no longer the other white meat."

That's right. Many breeds of pig have pink or red, rather than white meat. And heritage breeds now being revived by small farmers tend to have far more fat and more marbling in the meat than modern breeds.

When you're at the market, ask the farmer about his or her operation. What do the pigs eat? If the answer is acorns, you're in for a treat. Are the pigs free-range? It doesn't really jam with the common mental picture of immobile sows spending their days stretched out on beds of straw, but pigs like to move around. They have even been described as "frolicking." Ask about the breeds and cuts on offer.

You'll want to follow Russo's lead and use the various breeds in ways that will highlight their best characteristics. Lard breeds are good for curing and meat breeds want to be the centerpiece of the plate.

One of the most prized lard-type breeds is the Mangalitsa, a Hungarian hog prized for its fatty meat and often used for sausages. Farmers in the Upper Midwest are also raising many heritage breeds that are in demand for high-quality meat, including the Berkshire, Gloucestershire Old Spot, Duroc, and Red Wattle. Of these, the Berkshire is the fattiest, while the Red Wattle is leaner and has a flavor closest to beef.

At the farmers market, you'll have to choose among prewrapped cuts, because the farmer won't have the

WHEN TO FIND IT

Meat vendors will generally be at the market any time in the season. No matter when they butcher their animals, most meat producers will sell their products frozen at the market.

Minnesota is "pork central," according to Heartland chef Lenny Russo.

facilities to cut anything down for you, but you are likely to find a good variety. The shoulder, also known as the Boston butt, is good for long, slow cooking and for feeding a crowd. These come boneless or bone-in. This is what you want for shredded pork. Loin roasts and crown roasts are nice, big centerpieces for festive occasions. Chops are cut from the loin but are generally lean and cook quickly. The tenderloin is a long, thin, lean cut that cooks quickly (and is easy to overcook). It is tender and sweet and usually about a pound in weight. It's good for home curing and for loin and belly meat.

Once you've bought meat from a particular vendor a few times, if you've got the freezer space, consider talking with the farmer about buying a half or whole animal. You can have it processed however you like, usually at a very economical price per pound. You can expect prewrapped meat to keep in the freezer six to nine months.

A farmer selling pork is also likely to have tubs of creamy lard for sale. Leaf lard comes from the loin of the pig. It is snowy white and has a neutral flavor, which was why it was traditionally used in flaky pastries and other baked goods. The vendor may also have belly lard, which is darker in color and a good choice if you want to do some home preserving. Rillettes, for example, are a traditional form of pork cooked slowly in its own fat with plenty of spices, then potted and sealed with hardened fat.

The U.S. Department of Agriculture used to recommend cooking pork to an internal temperature of 160 degrees F to kill any possible food-borne illnesses. It recently lowered that recommendation to 145 degrees F, but some aficionados claim that is still too high and will ruin the flavor of some cuts.

GRILLED MINNESOTA PORK TENDERLOIN
with HEIRLOOM TOMATO-GREEN ONION RELISH

By Lenny Russo

Lenny Russo also serves this pork with the corn relish on page 68.

Pork

2 pounds boneless
naturally-raised pork
tenderloin, peeled
and trimmed

1 ounce fresh
rosemary, chopped

1 ounce fresh lavender,
chopped

2 tablespoons
grape seed oil

2 teaspoons fine
sea salt

½ teaspoon
black pepper,
freshly ground

Relish

4 heirloom tomatoes; peeled,
seeded, and diced ¼"

¼ cup green onions,
bias sliced ⅛"

1 teaspoon fresh
garlic, minced

2 tablespoons
fresh mint, chopped

2 tablespoons
apple cider vinegar

2 tablespoons grape seed oil

1 tablespoon walnut oil

1 teaspoon fine sea salt

½ teaspoon black pepper,
freshly ground

Brush the meat on both sides with the grape seed oil, and season it with salt, pepper, and herbs. Set aside. Meanwhile, dissolve the salt in the vinegar in a mixing bowl. Whisk in the oils. Add the tomatoes and onions along with the herbs. Mix well and set aside. Grill the pork over moderate heat for approximately 4 minutes on each side. Spoon some relish onto four serving plates, and place the pork on top of the relish. Serve immediately.

Serves four.

POTATOES

POTATOES SYMBOLIZE stodgy solidity and predictability—that's what it means to be a "meat-and-potatoes person," isn't it?—but there is more flavor and variety in the potato world than we are used to looking for. In Peru, ancestral home of the potato, there are thousands of varieties of potatoes, of all shapes, sizes, and hues. That range of variety has yet to make its way to Minnesota, but there are probably more kinds of potatoes than you expect at your local farmers market.

Purple potatoes, often a variety known as Purple Peruvian, are becoming quite common. The difference between their color and their flavor can be quite jarring—close your eyes and pop one in your mouth and it doesn't taste purple—but they can be used exactly like white-fleshed potatoes. They are especially nice when they can show off their lovely color—say, roasted in wedges, next to some coral-fleshed salmon—and less agreeable when that purple is unexpected or has a chance to turn a muddy brown—say, in potato pancakes. They tend to be starchy and so are particularly well suited to mashed potatoes.

Fingerlings are named for the long, elegant shape that causes some small farmers to curse them: They slip right through standard harvesting machinery. This is one reason you might find they cost a little more at the market. The other reason is their delicate, sought-after flavor.

The most important rule when at the market, says Steven Brown, chef and co-owner of Tilia restaurant in South Minneapolis, is to choose the right potato for the job. "You can't take a very waxy potato and expect to make a nice, smooth potato puree," he warns. Starchy potatoes, such as Russets, are the traditional choice for mashed potatoes and baking. Red potatoes tend to be waxy and are the best choice for potato salad, because

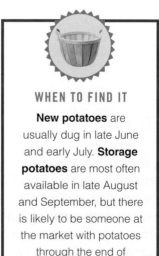

WHEN TO FIND IT

New potatoes are usually dug in late June and early July. **Storage potatoes** are most often available in late August and September, but there is likely to be someone at the market with potatoes through the end of the season.

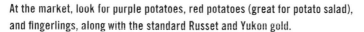

At the market, look for purple potatoes, red potatoes (great for potato salad), and fingerlings, along with the standard Russet and Yukon gold.

they don't fall apart. (Unless you like your potato salad, as some people do, with loose bits of mashed up potato holding it together. It's a matter of taste.)

You can also find a middle ground, with something like Yukon golds, which have a great buttery flavor and fall in the middle of the waxy-starchy spectrum. These are the workhorse potatoes in many kitchens. More common at farmers markets than at grocery stores are newer varieties of red-skinned potato with a yellow flesh, rather than white. These are also highly flavored and generally split the difference between starchy and waxy.

Your mother or grandmother probably told you to eat your potato peels "because that's where all the nutrition is." Well, additional fiber, vitamins, and minerals are in the peels, but the flesh is hardly devoid of nutrition and flavor, so go ahead and peel them, if you like. When boiling potatoes, it's best to cook them whole, in their skins. This will keep too much starch from coming off into the cooking water. But we've all been in a hurry to make mashed potatoes at some point and peeled and chopped the potatoes to significantly cut down on the cooking time, and the mashed potatoes—and the diners—survived. Either way, start them in cold water so that they cook more evenly.

Store potatoes in a cool, dark, dry place, such as a paper bag in the basement or garage. Do not keep potatoes in a plastic bag, as they will give off moisture and rot. And don't keep them in the fridge. At temperatures that low, potatoes start to convert their starches to sugar and get a strange, sweet, nonpotato flavor. Properly stored potatoes will keep for a couple of months, but certainly not forever, as we might want to think.

 True "new potatoes" are dug while the plant is still alive, usually in late June or early July.

If your potatoes do start to sprout, you can safely dig out any small eyes with a paring knife. You may have heard that a sprouted potato is poisonous and this is true to a certain extent—potato sprouts and plants do contain solanine, a poison found in species of the nightshade family—but it is not present in harmful amounts in the potatoes themselves. Any potatoes that have longer sprouts or have started to go soft should be discarded.

Potatoes that have been exposed to light either while they are growing or in storage may start to turn green in the layer of flesh just under the peel. You've probably heard that this is poisonous, too, and it is, mildly. Peel such potatoes deeply, cutting off all the green part, and they are safe to eat.

New potatoes are an eagerly awaited early summer treat. There are plenty of tiny spuds sold in the grocery store as "new potatoes," but true new potatoes are something different. Most potatoes are dug after the plant itself has died in the late summer and early fall. These are cured and will keep quite well. New potatoes are dug while the plant is still alive, usually in late June and early July. It's not the small size that is the badge of a true new potato—it is the skin. New potato skin will rub right off in your fingers, and they are therefore quite fragile and need to be used up almost immediately—within a week, at least.

New potatoes have such a lovely, summery flavor that you really don't need to do much with them: Boil them briefly (this will depend on their size, but it will be less than regular potatoes) and toss them with butter, maybe with some salt and chopped fresh dill. (Since new potatoes are particularly beloved in Scandinavia, this is a fitting accompaniment.)

POTATO CAULIFLOWER PUREE with AGRO DOLCE CIPOLLINIS

By Tilia Kitchen

This is among the most decadent mashed potato recipes out there. When you try it, you will understand why restaurant food can taste so much better than food we cook at home: Chefs aren't afraid of cream and butter, they're willing to boil a whole head of cauliflower just to flavor the potatoes, and they sweat the details. And it's all worth it.

Potato Puree

4 large russet potatoes, about 3 pounds, peeled and cut into 1½" chunks	Place potatoes in a pot of cold water. Gently boil until tender, about 45 minutes.
1 medium head of cauliflower	In a separate pot, gently simmer the cauliflower in the cream until tender, at least 20 minutes, or until the potatoes are done. (The cream will not cover the cauliflower; keep the lid on to keep it from boiling off.) Strain, reserving cream and discarding cauliflower.
1 pint heavy whipping cream	When potatoes are done, drain and push through a tamis or wire mesh strainer with the back of a spatula. Stir in melted butter, then add reserved cream, a little bit at a time, until the mixture is smooth and soft, but not runny. (You will use most of the cream, but probably not all.) Taste and add salt.
1½ cups melted unsalted butter	
Salt to taste	

Agro Dolce Cipollinis

Cipollinis are tiny onions about the size of a gumball. It takes a lot of patience to get their stubborn peels off. Two tricks that will help: Soak them in ice water about 30 minutes, or cut a small X in the tip and blanche them for about a minute.

A cartouche is a circle of parchment paper cut to the exact size of the top of your pan. It sits directly on top of the liquid you are cooking and controls the rate at which it thickens. You can also cook the onions with the pan's own lid on it, but you will need to keep a close eye on the rate at which the onions are cooking and the sauce is thickening. If the onions are going to be done before the sauce is thick enough, remove the lid for a few minutes.

1 ounce prosciutto, minced	Cook prosciutto in a sauté pan over medium heat until the fat renders out and the meat is crispy.
2 tablespoons sugar	Add sugar, stock, vinegar, and cider, and simmer until the sauce has reduced and is thick enough to coat the back of a spoon, about 5 minutes.
1 tablespoon chicken stock	
1 tablespoon apple cider vinegar	
1 tablespoon apple cider	Add cipollinis, top with cartouche, and cook on low heat, until cipollinis are tender and liquid coats the onions, about 25 minutes. Add additional chicken stock as needed, if liquid becomes too reduced.
1 pound cipollini onions, peeled	
2 tablespoons unsalted butter	
1 tablespoon soy sauce	Remove from heat and stir in butter and soy sauce, adjusting flavor with additional vinegar and salt, if necessary.
Salt to taste	

RADISHES

THE BUNCHES OF RADISHES you might see on the tables at many farmers markets are almost too pretty to eat: The bundles of bright red or variegated purple, pink, and white look like happy balloons. If your experience with radishes begins and ends at the grocery store or buffet garnishes, then you might be surprised with the variety of colors, shapes, and flavors.

Those beautiful clusters of red, purple, pink, and white radishes are known as Easter egg radishes. French breakfast radishes are elongated with a red top fading to a white tip. They are mildly peppery. White icicle radishes, on the other hand, have a similar shape but a strong bite. Daikon radishes are long, like carrots, sometimes even bigger than carrots, and very, very mild. Black radishes have a thick, rough black skin and a white interior and are slightly less peppery than your average red globe.

The flavor of all of these radishes, however, is affected by the weather, getting sharper as it gets hotter.

What do most people do with radishes? Pretty much one thing: They eat them raw. Maybe sliced, maybe in a salad. Maybe carved into roses and arranged around a vegetable platter. That's it. But radishes are transformed when you roast them. They get sweet and crisp and nutty. French breakfast radishes are especially good when roasted (twenty minutes at 400 degrees F will do the trick) and then bathed in salted butter.

Radish tops are, indeed, edible, but they often look in rough shape because radishes aren't often bred for their tops. If the tops are sunburnt, bruised, tough, or very, very limp, give them a pass. But if they look like they're in good shape, you're in for a treat. Radish greens have a strong peppery flavor and will make a powerful pesto, or can be stirred into soup to give it a kick. If you sauté your radishes, add the tops halfway through cooking for a double-radish dish. Baby radish greens are often found in salad mixes; however, once they're mature, they are a little too scratchy

WHEN TO FIND IT

Radishes are in it for the long haul. They can be ready to harvest in as little as a month after planting. So some farmers will have them on the market's opening day and will stagger plantings so they can harvest them until the first frost.

132

Pack-Shot/Shutterstock.com

✺
French breakfast radishes are mildly peppery; their flavor gets sharper as the weather gets hotter.

✷

1. Daikon radishes are very, very mild. 2. For a change of pace, roast radishes and brush them with salted butter.

to eat raw in salads. Radish greens tend to trap lots of dirt, so swish them around in plenty of cool water before cooking.

At the market, look for radishes with the greens attached, even if you don't intend to eat them. The tops are a good way to gauge how fresh the radishes themselves are. Don't worry about a little dirt clinging to the roots, but be wary of any signs of splitting or any particularly hard spots. These are signs that the radishes are a bit too mature and have gotten woody.

At home, cut the tops off and store them separately (if you intend to eat them). The greens will keep in a plastic bag, wrapped loosely in a paper towel, for about a week. The roots will keep for a couple of weeks in a plastic bag. It is generally best to wait to wash vegetables until just before you plan to eat them, yet a bowl of washed and trimmed radishes in the fridge, just ready and waiting to be popped into your mouth, is a great thing to have in the summer. They'll dry out a little this way, but the convenience is worth it.

DAIKON RADISH PICKLES

By Carrie Boyd

Daikon radishes are definitely one of those vegetables that might have you asking, "What do I do with it?" As manager of the Onamia Area Farmers Market, Carrie Boyd has this answer for you.

1½ daikon radishes, peeled and cut into ¼" slices
¾ teaspoon salt
1 tablespoon rice vinegar
¼ teaspoon ground black pepper
1 tablespoon sesame oil

Toss the daikon with the salt in a bowl. Cover and refrigerate for about 30 minutes, until they have released some liquid. Drain and pat dry. Stir together remaining ingredients and toss with radishes. Cover and refrigerate at least 8 hours.

RAMPS and FIDDLEHEADS

RAMPS AND FIDDLEHEADS are, of course, two completely separate plants. What joins them is all that they have in common. They are the harbingers of spring, among the first things to appear in the markets. And when they are gone—as they will be in a flash—they are very much gone for good, not to appear again until the next spring.

Ramps and fiddleheads, along with many mushrooms, including morels, are so unchangeably seasonal because they are exclusively wild and uncultivated. What you see in the markets will be foraged. As such, farmers can't eke out a longer growing season with hoop houses or staggered plantings or the like. When it comes to ramps and fiddleheads, we take what we can get.

Ramps are also known as wild leeks. They are, however, much smaller than any leek you have ever seen, about as thick as a pencil or even skinnier. The base is a narrow white bulb with a bit of pink at the top, fading into dark green, narrow leaves. The whole plant is edible, with a mild garlicky flavor and a delicate hint of lemon.

Ramps make the most delicious pesto. You can puree the whole plant with olive oil (no need for garlic!) or cook the white bulbs gently first. They are also lovely sautéed, as an accompaniment with dinner, although a whole dish of ramps on the side might be a bit much. They go beautifully with eggs, as in a frittata. And there are people who lie in wait for ramps just so they can pickle them. You can pickle them using your favorite cucumber recipe, or you can make a quick refrigerator pickle with a light-flavored vinegar, salt, and spices.

At the market, look for fairly uniformly sized bundles, with firm bulbs and fresh, crisp leaves. Inspect the tiny white roots at the base: Do they still look moist and fresh or have they dried out?

Ramps will keep just a few days in the fridge in a plastic bag.

Fiddleheads are the young tops of any of a number of different varieties of fern. These are the leaves, still curled

WHEN TO FIND IT

Fiddleheads and **ramps** are the first green things to come up out of the ground, usually in May. Come early June, they're almost always gone.

135

like—yes—a fiddle that will unfurl into fronds. Before they uncurl, they are tender and taste earthy. In Minnesota, the most common kind of fern to be harvested for fiddleheads is the ostrich fern. You should look out, however, for bracken ferns, which are believed to be carcinogenic.

All fiddleheads should be cooked thoroughly before eating, because they are likely to harbor toxic bacteria (bad enough to give you a pretty tough stomachache). Remove any yellow or brown parts and boil the fiddleheads for five minutes and then rinse and drain them thoroughly before using in your recipe.

Once you've boiled your fiddleheads, you can use them just like that, tossed with olive oil, vinegar, salt, and pepper and served as a side dish. You can also pat them

David Kay/Shutterstock.com

✳
Ramps (also called wild leeks) are among the first greens to appear in spring.

GRILLED RAMPS

The fresh, delicate flavor of ramps needs little adornment. You may be tempted later in the season to try fancier preparations, but here's what you want to do with your first bunch of ramps.

1 bunch of ramps
1 tablespoon olive oil
Salt and pepper to taste
1 tablespoon balsamic vinegar
   or lemon juice

Heat a grill on high or griddle pan over medium-high heat. Trim roots from ramps and toss with oil, salt, and pepper. Use your hands to be sure the oil coats them all evenly. Carefully arrange the ramps on the grill (perpendicular to the racks, it stands to reason) and cook about 1 minute on each side. Remove to a serving platter and drizzle with balsamic vinegar or lemon juice.

*
Fiddleheads (the young, unfurled tops of ferns) are also an early spring delicacy.

FIDDLEHEADS AND BACON

By Carrie Boyd

Carrie Boyd recommends applewood-smoked bacon for this decadent preparation of fiddlehead ferns.

½ pound fiddlehead ferns	Boil fiddleheads for 5 minutes, then drain and plunge into very cold water. Cook the bacon over medium heat. Remove from pan and drain off all but a tablespoon or two of the fat. Add the onions and cook over medium-high until crispy and brown. Reserve.
12 ounces bacon, cut into 1" pieces	
1 medium onion, chopped	In a separate pan, heat 1 tablespoon of the butter over medium-high heat and sauté the ferns for about 3 minutes, being careful not to scorch the butter. Add the garlic and cook, stirring and keeping a close eye on it, until the garlic is brown. Add the wine and simmer until it is almost entirely cooked off. Remove from heat and stir in remaining tablespoon of butter. Taste and add salt and pepper as needed.
1 large clove garlic	
¼ cup dry white wine	
2 tablespoons butter, divided	
Salt and pepper	Remove the fiddleheads to a serving platter and top with crisped onions and bacon.

dry and add them to a stir-fry, pasta dish, or frittata. You can also pickle fiddleheads, but boil and rinse them first. A recipe for dilly beans—with dill seed and mustard—works well with these ferns.

Plan to use your fiddleheads the day you buy them or the next. Their texture and flavor deteriorate quickly. Keep them in a plastic bag with some holes punched in it in the fridge.

RHUBARB

T HE WORLD CAN be divided fairly neatly into two camps: Those who love the puckery sour-sweetness of rhubarb and those who will never understand the appeal. The former are happy to peel the toughest strings from a pink and green stalk, dip it in sugar, and eat it just like that—which makes the latter shake their heads.

Rhubarb is the quintessential early-summer flavor. It is one of the few fruits and vegetables left that is almost impossible to find outside of its local growing season: the last seasonal treats. Farmers usually harvest in May and June and then stop so the plant can put its energy back into growing for the next year. (Rhubarb is a notoriously hardy perennial.) Some growers will harvest a second time in August, but you can't really count on finding it in the markets then.

Rhubarb loves the company of other early-summer favorites, such as strawberries. The sweet-tart-earthy combination of the two is so natural that it almost seems like it must be more than just coincidence that they ripen together just as we start longing for fresher flavors. But rhubarb is also at home in savory dishes: in chutneys alongside pork and chicken, in salads with earthy beets, and on appetizers with tangy cheeses, just for a start.

Fanatics notwithstanding, rhubarb is almost always eaten cooked. Before cooking, peel off just the toughest outer strings; don't bother peeling stalks completely. Rhubarb cooks down quite a bit: A pound turns into about three-quarters of a cup when cooked. To make a simple sauce, simmer chunks of rhubarb in a covered saucepan with sugar (how much depends entirely on your sour-tooth) and just a tiny bit of water to keep it from sticking. Within ten to fifteen minutes, the pieces will have completely disintegrated. You can use the sauce as is, or strain out the pulp for something a little more refined. This liquid can be reduced to intensify the flavor; or you can cook it down to a syrupy consistency to make a gastrique—equally good on grilled meats and ice cream.

WHEN TO FIND IT
Rhubarb is in the market in May and June.

Diana Taljun/Shutterstock.com

✴
Rhubarb is most often used in desserts, but it's also delicious in savory dishes.

At the market, look for rhubarb with the leaves already trimmed off. If for some reason the farmer did leave the leaves on, trim them off as soon as you get home and wash the stalks well. The leaves contain high levels of oxalates and are poisonous. Look for bright pink stalks that fade to green, are too crisp to bend, and don't look dried out. In a plastic bag in the fridge, you can expect rhubarb stalks to keep for two to four weeks, though they won't taste as fresh. If the stalks get floppy, you can reinvigorate them in a cold-water bath.

Rhubarb freezes beautifully. It's as easy as cutting it into manageable pieces (say, one-inch) and putting it in plastic bags with as much air squeezed out as possible. It will be soft and mushy and ready for cooking when you thaw it out. With a few extra steps, you can preserve rhubarb's bright pink color as well as its flavor when freezing: Cut it into pieces, blanch it for one minute in boiling water, transfer immediately to a bowl of ice water to shock it, drain well, and freeze.

RHUBARB JUICE AND JELLY

By Gail Rixen

Gail Rixen raises crops and sheep on Kroeger and Rixen Farm and sells them, along with pickles and jellies, at Bemidji Natural Choice Farmers Market. She also likes to use the liquid from this recipe to make juice for drinking (adding ½–¾ cup sugar to a quart of liquid).

About 4 pounds rhubarb, washed and cut into large chunks
2 cups water
1 package liquid pectin (Sure-Jell is recommended)
6 cups sugar (or as directed)

Place rhubarb and water in a large stockpot. Cover and cook on low at least 1 hour, until the rhubarb has turned completely to mush. Be careful not to cook off too much liquid. Strain through gauze or a jelly bag, being sure not to squeeze the bag. (That would cloud the jelly.) It's best to leave it to hang overnight.

Use 4 cups of rhubarb juice, pectin, and 6 cups sugar to make jelly according to package directions.

RHUBARB-BLUEBERRY COBBLER

By Carol Whitcomb

Carol Whitcomb and her husband, Dan, grow apples, blueberries, and raspberries at J. Q. Fruit Farm & Orchard in Princeton. This cobbler recipe can be used with just about any combination of fruit or berries, but sweet blueberries and tart rhubarb are an unexpected combination. While rhubarb and blueberries usually aren't ripe at the same time, you can pull one or the other, or both, from your freezer to make this just about any time.

2 cups chopped rhubarb, fresh or frozen
2 cups blueberries, fresh or frozen
¼ cup tapioca
3 tablespoons plus 1 cup of sugar, divided
1¼ cups unsalted butter, melted and cooled
1½ cups flour
2 eggs
Pinch of salt

Preheat oven to 350°F.
Stir together rhubarb, blueberries, tapioca, and
    3 tablespoons of the sugar and allow to sit for
    10 minutes. Pour fruit mixture into a 9x9" pan.
Mix together remaining ingredients in a separate
    bowl and dollop it over the fruit. It may not
    completely cover the fruit.
Bake 45 minutes, until topping begins to brown.
    Serve warm.

ROOT VEGETABLES (RUTABAGAS, TURNIPS, CELERY ROOT, and SUNCHOKES)

I F YOU FIND FALL root vegetables unfamiliar and baffling, you're not alone. Turnips and rutabagas are often big and unwieldy; they're hard and seem to need forever to cook. Celery root can be shaggy, dirty, and mottled green. And sunchokes look like—well, like nothing else in the market. They're knobby and woody on the outside, like bloated ginger root. Once you get past their looks, however, there is plenty of delicious local flavor to be unlocked in these fall vegetables.

Rutabagas and turnips are like siblings who are constantly being mistaken for one another. In fact, what Americans call a rutabaga or a Swede (to the great amusement of the rest of Scandinavia) is called a turnip in some other English-speaking countries.

The difference is almost moot. Anything you can do with a turnip, you can do with a rutabaga. Both are purple on the outside (the rutabaga tends to be darker), while the turnip is white on the inside and the rutabaga is yellow in the inside. Rutabagas tend to have more bitter notes than turnips, but there are variations among varieties as well.

Cubed and boiled, turnips and rutabagas add a little sweetness to chicken soup. Many who make their own chicken broth also swear by including a turnip along with the other vegetables.

In Scotland and northern Europe, turnips and rutabagas are often served boiled and mashed, either mixed roughly half and half with potatoes or on their own. If your root vegetables are small, they are also prime candidates for salt roasting (see page 35).

WHEN TO FIND IT

Root vegetables start appearing in the market in September and will stick around through the end of the market season. Connoisseurs look for the ones harvested after the first frost. Some vendors who overwinter their root vegetables and use passive solar technology, such as high hoops, will have them first thing in the spring as well.

141

1: Brzostowska/Shutterstock.com; 2: iStockphoto.com/sdstockphoto; 3: Tim Stirling/Shutterstock.com; 4: Bobkeenan Photography/Shutterstock.com

✸

1. Celeriac (or celery root). 2. Rutabagas. 3. Sunchokes (Jerusalem artichokes). 4. Turnips.

Turnips can even be eaten raw. Cut them into matchstick-sized sticks (julienne) and toss them with a strong-flavored vinaigrette. Rutabagas aren't as tasty that way, however.

The leaves of both turnips and rutabagas are edible, but you won't find them still attached to the vegetables in the late fall, however, when they will have already died off. If you find young vegetables with the tops attached, wash them well and sauté them.

Hakurei turnips, also called Japanese turnips or salad turnips, are something else entirely. These are available in the early summer and are more like radishes, with small, nearly spherical, pure white bulbs. They are tasty raw, whether in salads or sprinkled with salt. You can also sauté them with their greens.

Celery root, or celeriac, is the root of a celery plant, a close cousin of the celery you eat for the tops. It tastes of celery, lemon, and radish, and it looks just ferocious. Its outside is gnarled and nobbled and covered in little roots, often packed with dirt. To get to the good stuff inside, you need to cut a flat base and stand it on your cutting board, then work your way around it with a knife, taking a good quarter inch off the outside. It tends to brown quickly when exposed to air, so it's good to have some lemon juice on hand.

Celery root can also be mashed with potatoes or cubed and added to soups. It also makes a lovely smooth soup: Cook it with a little butter, garlic, onions, and salt. Cover it with water or broth and boil until it's soft. Then puree. It's that easy.

But celery root gets to take its star turn in remoulade, a condiment made from the grated root, mustard, mayonnaise, horseradish, and lemon. Serve it alongside a roast on your holiday table, or spread it on a sandwich.

Sunchokes are also known as Jerusalem artichokes, not because they are any relation to the artichoke, but because that's the closest analogue for their flavor. They're actually the roots of a plant in the daisy family. Inside their woody skin, they should be crisp and even slightly juicy, not dense like other root vegetables.

The skin is edible but can be a little tough in larger roots, so it's up to you if you peel them or not. One easy way to serve them is to slice them and toss them with a little olive oil and salt, then roast them in a 450-degree oven for about fifteen minutes. They should turn out brown and crispy. You can peel, boil, and puree sunchokes, but they are so watery and mild-flavored, not to mention low on starch, that those techniques are rarely satisfying. Sunchokes are, however, prime candidates for salt roasting, since they are smaller and easier to cover in salt. If you're not afraid of the deep-fryer, thinly sliced sunchokes make delicious chips. You can also peel them, slice them, and brine them overnight in a mixture of vinegar and spices.

At the market, look for smooth, bruise-free vegetables. A little dirt—or a lot, in the case of celeriac—still clinging to them is okay. Root vegetables are usually cured after harvesting, meaning they are kept in a cool dry place until the cut at the top where the greens were removed has healed, so it's normal not to see a fresh cut at the stem side.

SLOW-ROASTED GARLIC WINTER ROOT VEGETABLE GRATIN

By David Brauer

Adapted from Deborah Madison's **Vegetarian Cooking for Everyone**

After decades of dogged hard work as a journalist in the Twin Cities, David Brauer found a new passion on the board of the Kingfield and Fulton farmers markets in Minneapolis. He now works just as tirelessly promoting local food and strong communities. He's also a pretty good cook.

This isn't a traditional gratin in that it isn't drowning in cream. Instead the garlic, oil, and flour make a powerfully flavorful crust that just holds the veggies together. Brauer makes this with just about any combination of root vegetables, including peeled and cubed butternut squash, parsnips, and carrots. In fact, this should be your go-to recipe when you've got fall and winter vegetables and are wondering what to do with them.

2–2½ pounds root vegetables, peeled cut into 1" cubes

5–10 garlic cloves, chopped

½ cup chopped parsley

¾ teaspoon kosher salt

¾ teaspoon freshly ground pepper

3 tablespoons flour

¼–½ cup extra virgin olive oil, plus more to oil the pan

½ cup chopped parsley

Preheat oven to 325°F. Oil shallow glass or earthenware baking dish. (A 9x13" pan works well.)

In a large bowl, toss root vegetables with garlic, parsley, salt, and pepper. Add flour until pieces are lightly coated; don't worry if some falls to the bottom. Pile the mixture evenly into the dish and drizzle oil generously over the top. Bake, uncovered, until the mix is tender and the top is browned, about 2 hours.

SALAD GREENS

THE GEMS OF the early summer farmers markets are the leafy greens: fat, juicy heads of red and green lettuces, bushel baskets full of mixed baby greens, and a tempting trail of other greens you might not even recognize. And, as anyone who has ever picked up a head of lettuce at the farmers market in the morning and eaten it that same day knows: These are so different from commercial lettuces in the grocery store.

Perhaps more than any other vegetable we might buy, lettuces and other salad greens illustrate the remarkable differences between plants grown for sturdiness, storage, and travel and those grown for flavor. Freshly picked lettuce still tastes alive, still tastes *green* and earthy, sweet and complex.

Enjoy these gems while you can, however, because lettuce hates the heat and will disappear from the market (or decline markedly in quality, getting tougher and more bitter) until September brings cooler weather.

The array of greens available at the market can truly be staggering or inspiring, however you see it. From delicate, creamy butter head lettuce (also known as Bibb, Boston, or Boston Bibb) to sharp, peppery arugula.

Beyond their color, red and green leaf lettuces are interchangeable, with little difference in flavor. These are the workhorses of the summer salad season, versatile crowd pleasers that can take just about any dressing.

Romaine, thanks to the Caesar salad craze of the past few decades, may have become the new iceberg lettuce: ubiquitous and beloved for its sturdiness rather than its flavor. Iceberg, in fact, is the one lettuce you may never see at a Minnesota farmers market. Not only is it wildly out of fashion, it prefers California's temperate Central Valley to our climate.

When it comes to two other families of salad greens, endives and chicories, we get a little tangled up in our

WHEN TO FIND IT

Salad greens are likely to be at your market the first day it opens, thanks to greenhouses and passive solar techniques, and again when it cools down in the fall. Tougher greens, especially **mustard greens**, may be there all summer long but will be more bitter in hot weather.

1. Red and green leaf lettuce. 2. Mizuna. 3. Escarole (a type of endive).

terminology. In fact, one of the most common chicories is the one we call "Belgian endive." This is the elongated white one with yellow tips and it is particularly, deliciously bitter. Belgian endive's Italian cousin and fellow chicory, radicchio—a petite cabbage-shaped purple ball—is milder. Neither is closely related to curly endive (frisée), the lacy one that the French like to dress up as *frisée aux lardons*, with big bites of bacon and a soft-boiled egg.

The other common type of endive—and one that loves Minnesota's climate—is escarole. Escarole is easily mistaken for lettuce, but look for wide, white ribs and sturdy, deeply fanned leaves. Escarole is beloved in Italy and tastes even better cooked than raw.

Farmers markets are great places to look for less common greens, such as delicate, juicy mache (also known as lamb's lettuce or corn lettuce) and watercress.

You'll also likely find a wide variety of things labeled "mustard greens," especially in the stalls of Hmong and Vietnamese farmers. These might include mizuna—a frizzy, delicate, peppery green—and tatsoi, which is more similar to spinach. If any of these look good, go ahead and ask the vender how they like to eat them—raw? Steamed? Pickled? It's a great way to discover new favorites.

You've probably had a salad of baby greens in a restaurant or bought a pack of mixed baby greens. These are just any sort of leafy vegetable, from lettuce to beet tops, picked young. But what's smaller than baby greens? Micro greens, of course. These are tiny—like the head of a Q-tip tiny—and packed with flavor. Elizabeth Millard and Karla Pankow grow micro greens on their farm, Bossy Acres, in southern Minnesota, and sell mixes with as many as eighteen varieties of greens at Twin Cities farmers markets.

"You know that moment in *Willie Wonka* where Violet is chewing the gum?" Millard says, trying to describe the flavor. "It's like that. A beet top *that* small, and it tastes like the whole beet."

Micro greens are a great way for farmers to make use of the tops of plants as they thin them out, and they put pizzazz into everyday salads.

You may hear that you should never wash lettuce until you're ready to use it. And this is, generally speaking, pretty good advice. Rough washing and excess moisture in the storage container can cause greens to decline in quality more quickly, but the truth is that the biggest barrier to actually making a salad is having to pull out the salad spinner. So if it makes it more likely that you will make that salad for Tuesday dinner, go ahead and wash your farmers market lettuce on Saturday afternoon.

Start by filling up the largest pot or bowl you've got with cool water. (You could do this in your—very clean— sink, but you'll be sending all the grit on the leaves down your drain.) Swish the leaves gently, in small batches, and then leave them alone for a minute, so the grit can settle to the bottom. Move the leaves to a salad spinner and repeat. Store dry greens wrapped loosely in a paper or cloth kitchen towel in a closed plastic bag or plastic container, but be careful not to cram them in.

Don't freeze your greens! Keep them away from the coldest parts of your fridge or you may find them limp and rotten-looking, the result of having frozen and thawed as your fridge cycled on and off. Also, it's best not to let greens sit out at room temperature for more than thirty minutes or so, or they'll dry out and go limp. Most of the time you can revive them with a good cool-water bath.

You may have heard that you should always tear never cut—lettuce, because tearing allows the lettuce to break along its natural cell lines and this will keep it from browning as quickly. It turns out this is true, but only relevant if you're going to keep

---

BABY MIXED GREENS AND PEAR SALAD
By Faye Carroll

Faye Carroll is a vendor at the Mora Area Farmers Market, where she sells her vegetables, eggs, preserves, and pickles. She also likes to make this salad with baby spinach.

---

4 cups mixed baby greens or spinach
1 large fresh pear, sliced thinly
⅓ cup shaved Parmesan cheese
2 tablespoons balsamic vinegar
1 tablespoon mustard
1 teaspoon sugar
1 teaspoon salt
¼ teaspoon black pepper
½ cup extra virgin olive oil

Arrange greens or spinach on salad plate, arrange pear slices on top and sprinkle shaved cheese on pears. Whisk together remaining ingredients and drizzle on salad.

Serves four.

BRAISED ESCAROLE

Cooked greens? Absolutely. This classic Italian dish is somewhere between a soup and side—in any case, it definitely needs to be served in bowls.

1 clove garlic, minced

1 shallot, thinly sliced

1 tablespoon olive oil

1 head escarole, washed and roughly chopped

2 cups cooked cannellini beans
    (or 1 16-ounce can, drained)

2 cups unsalted chicken or vegetable broth or water

¼ teaspoon freshly grated nutmeg

¼ cup freshly grated Parmesan

Salt and pepper to taste

Cook garlic and shallot in olive oil over medium heat until soft. Add escarole and cook, stirring, for a couple of minutes until it wilts and starts to brown. Add beans, broth, and nutmeg and simmer, uncovered, 10 minutes. Stir in Parmesan. Taste and add salt and pepper as needed.

Serves four.

the lettuce around for days. In the time it takes to get the lettuce from your cutting board to your plate, it won't make a difference.

When it's time to dress the leaves, make sure they are completely dry. Dry leaves will take dressing better and you'll be able to coat them more evenly and use less dressing. You should probably use less dressing than you think; about a tablespoon for every two cups. Start with the leaves in a large bowl with plenty of room for tossing. Then toss and toss, and toss some more.

Salads are terrific, but you can also think beyond the salad bowl. Romaine is fantastic grilled. Cut it in half lengthwise, keeping the stem intact so it stays together, and put it on a hot grill until charred. This brings out flavor you never knew you could find in romaine.

When your lettuce is headed south (but not rotten), braise it with a flavorful broth or cook it in a creamy, pureed soup. Endive is often cooked in a cheesy sauce for the classic French dish *endives au gratin.*

SPINACH and OTHER DARK LEAFY GREENS

FOR MANY PEOPLE, dark leafy greens are a tougher sell than lettuce and other salad greens. They're more assertive in flavor, often a little bitter, and they usually need a little more prep than just tossing into a salad bowl. The phrase "Eat your spinach!" conjures up feelings of nutritional obligation, rather than pleasure.

That's really too bad, but for those in the know it just means, "More for us."

In recent years, kale has reached something like celebrity vegetable status, and it is well deserved. Curly kale was once best known for covering the edges of all-you-can-eat buffets (because that stuff is nearly indestructible), but its close relative lacinato, or dinosaur, kale is a sleek, dark, sometimes almost black, beauty with a rich, deep flavor. It is best braised but can be baked (just until it wilts or into crispy chips) or even—if young, fresh, and sliced thin—be eaten raw.

The classic Italian trio, kale with white beans and sausage, is a great combination in a soup, tossed with pasta, or in a braised stew on its own. Because it is a little bitter, kale also loves sweet vegetables, such as turnips, winter squash, and sweet potatoes.

Kale is an excellent gateway into the world of dark, leafy greens, but it will probably never usurp the place of familiar spinach. For salads, baby spinach is a better bet—more tender and less astringent. (You know how spinach can make it feel like your teeth have dried out? That's oxalic acid, which is actually toxic, but you'd have to eat thousands of pounds of spinach before it killed you.) As a matter of taste, mature spinach is better cooked. It does cook down into almost nothing: A pound of spinach will yield about one cup, so plan accordingly. Spinach has enough water in it that you don't need to add any liquid

WHEN TO FIND IT

Some kind of **dark leafy green** is sure to be available throughout the market season. Look for **chard** and **spinach** in the early summer and early fall, in the months bracketing the really hot season. **Collards** don't mind the heat and will come in July and August. Some growers will wait until after the frost to harvest **kale**, but its current popularity is sure to bring it to the market earlier than that.

1: Lauraslens/Shutterstock.com; 2: Jerry-Rainey/Shutterstock.com

1. Lacinato kale (also called dinosaur kale). 2. A chard stem makes a great garnish for a Bloody Mary.

to the pan when you cook it: Just give it a few turns in a little oil in the bottom of a hot pan to keep it from sticking, put the lid on, and it will steam in a minute or so.

For most people, collards are either (a) a beloved part of your culinary heritage or (b) completely foreign and a little intimidating. Strangely enough, here in Minnesota, where they aren't necessarily part of the local culinary culture, collards grow well. The big, round leaves—sometimes literally "as big as your head"—can be tough or tender, depending on how old they are. They are milder in flavor than other dark, leafy greens.

The standard approach in the American South is to cook the bejeezus out of them, up to three hours, along with a flavorful bit of pork. This yields a soupy, silky dish wherein the liquid, the "potlikker," is just as coveted as the greens themselves. But when sliced into long, thin ribbons, collard greens can also be sautéed in hot, flavorful oil (say, with garlic and hot peppers) for just a few minutes.

According to Karla Pankow, who farms at Bossy Acres, some people even like to use collard greens as alternatives to tortillas. It's best to blanch and dry them first.

It's easy to recognize the tangy, earthy flavor of chard when you know that it is actually a variety of beet, grown for its full, leafy tops rather than for the root itself. Swiss chard has ivory-colored stems and in other English-speaking countries has the more poetic name "silverbeet." It is distinguished from rainbow chard more by color than by flavor. Bunches of rainbow chard have white, yellow, and red stems. When you buy them, you should thank your farmer for the extra effort: Each plant only grows in one color, so to get the rainbow effect, leaves from a number of plants need to be bunched together.

The tops of red, golden, and Chioggia beets are also edible and are delightfully sweet and tangy when cooked. They cook up like spinach and are a nice alternative. Turnip greens are a more acquired taste, a little more bitter, but just as easy to cook.

Fresh kale, chard, and collards are not floppy, so look for bunches that practically stand up on their own when you hold them vertically. They should also look slightly glossy on the surface, rather than dried out.

Wash dark, leafy greens as you would salad greens, keeping in mind that spinach and kale can be especially gritty and need some extra swishing to get the dirt out of the myriad puckers in their surface. Store them wrapped loosely in a paper or cloth kitchen towel in a plastic bag or other container. They will keep up to two weeks, which is longer than more delicate greens.

To stem or not to stem? It depends on the green. Remove and discard the stems of kale, collards, and mature spinach leaves. Baby spinach can be eaten stems and all. The stems of chard and beet tops are edible, but need extra cooking time, so you should remove them and cook them separately. Chard stems, in particular, are terrific when chopped and tossed with a quick pickling mixture (vinegar, sugar, water, and spices) and left in the fridge for a day or two. Or leave the stems long when you pickle them and you'll have one of the best garnishes for a Bloody Mary ever.

SESAME KALE

By Atina Diffley

Atina Diffley notes that this recipe may serve just two, "depending on appetite and level of kale passion" (for her, that's high), and she says the level of garlic should be adjusted "according to your taste and social life."

1 bunch of organic kale, stems removed
 and coarsely chopped
1 to 4 cloves of garlic, minced
1 tablespoon olive oil
1/4 cup water
Roasted sesame oil
Ume plum vinegar

Heat olive oil in a heavy pan. Sauté garlic for 20 to 30 seconds, stirring. Mix in chopped kale. Add water and cover. Steam on low for 5 to 10 minutes, until desired tenderness. Spread on platter. Sprinkle with roasted sesame oil and Ume plum vinegar to taste.

Serves four.

KALE PESTO

Courtesy of the Mill City Farmers Market

You can substitute chard in this recipe (and go ahead and use the chard stems) for a tangier taste. Use this to dress up pasta or pizza. Spread on sandwiches (grilled cheese, especially) or drizzle over grilled meats.

2 cups kale, ribs removed, and chopped
¼ cup Parmesan cheese, shredded
¼ cup almonds
3 cloves garlic
2 teaspoons lemon juice
¼ cup olive oil
Salt and pepper to taste

Add the kale, cheese, almonds, garlic, and lemon juice to a food processor and pulse until combined. Slowly add the olive oil and then season to taste.

WINTER SQUASH and PUMPKINS

THANK GOODNESS FOR winter squash. When the last of the green vegetables have disappeared from the markets, the tables fill up with colorful squashes. The range and variety of squashes can be exhilarating, from the sweet little acorn squashes to the outsized and ghostly blue (and very squashy-tasting) Hubbard. And, of course, here's everybody's favorite, the pumpkin, which seems like a thing apart but is actually just another type of winter squash.

You know those cans of pumpkin pie filling on grocery shelves? You know what's in there? It might well be pumpkin, but it's just as likely to be butternut squash. Has that ever affected the quality of your pumpkin pie? Nope. Take note of that when you want to make your favorite pumpkin bread, pumpkin pie, or pumpkin anything else recipe and a host of squashes are staring at you from the counter, waiting to be used up.

To make a squash puree to use in those recipes, take your squash—just about any kind will do—cut it in half (lengthwise for a butternut, through the equator for more spherical varieties), scoop out the seeds, and put each half cut side down on a rimmed baking sheet (a layer of aluminum foil or parchment paper will make cleanup easier). Put these in a 400-degree oven until you can easily make an impression in the skin of the squash with your finger. This will take anywhere between twenty and forty minutes. Scoop the cooked flesh from the skin and puree in a food processor or blender. This keeps well in the freezer.

Be careful when slicing into the hard exterior of a squash. Always use a sharp knife (dull knives are far more dangerous) and take your time. For especially tough specimens, use a rubber mallet to tap a meat cleaver or large, heavy chef's knife gently but firmly through the flesh.

Remember the roasted pumpkin seeds you loved as a kid or the pepitas in your favorite Mexican dishes? Just about any kind of squash seed will be delicious roasted. Turban and kabocha squashes tend to have seeds with tough outer shells, however. When you scoop out the

WHEN TO FIND IT

Squash starts showing up in the markets in September and is available through the end of the season.

PUMPKIN SOUP

By Mary Helmerick

This soup, created by Mary Helmerick of the City of White Bear Lake Farmers Market, is like everything that's great about Thanksgiving in one warm bowl. It is delicious with turkey in place of the chicken.

1 12-ounce bag of fresh cranberries

¾ cup sugar

2 tablespoons plus ¼ cup butter, divided

1 medium onion

1 clove garlic

1 small rutabaga, cut into ½" cubes

1 butternut squash, peeled and cut into ½" cubes

2 medium carrots, peeled and cut into fat half-moons

10 cups vegetable or chicken broth, divided

½ cup flour

½ teaspoon salt

2 cups cooked wild rice

4 chicken breasts, cooked and cut into bite-sized pieces

4 cups cooked pumpkin or 2 15-ounce cans of pumpkin

4 cups half and half

¼ teaspoon pepper

⅛ teaspoon cayenne pepper

1 tablespoon pumpkin seasoning (ground cloves, nutmeg, and ginger)

Simmer cranberries with sugar in a cup of water for 10 minutes. Set aside.

Melt butter in a large stock pot over medium heat and cook onions and garlic until translucent. Add rutabaga, squash, carrots, and 8 cups of the broth. Bring to a boil and simmer until vegetables are soft.

Meanwhile, in a separate pan, make a soup base: Melt remaining ¼ cup butter over medium-high heat, stir in flour and salt, and cook, stirring, about 1 minute, until mixture smells nutty. Stir in remaining 2 cups of broth. Bring to a boil and simmer until mixture is about as thick as heavy cream.

Add this soup base to the stock pot, along with cooked cranberries and all remaining ingredients.

Reduce heat to low and simmer until warm.

seeds, put them in some water to soak for a half hour or so. This will make it easier to separate the seeds from the pulp for roasting. Pat them mostly dry on a kitchen towel, toss with salt, spread on a baking sheet, and cook until they're toasty brown, about fifteen minutes.

For some uses, squash varieties are pretty much interchangeable, but not for all. Delicata squashes are small and sausage-shaped. These are among the few winter squashes with edible skins. Slicing them and frying them makes a nice side dish; baking the halves with herbs and butter makes a hearty vegetarian main dish.

Butternut squashes are ideal for dishes in which you want nice, smooth cubes that hold their shape when cooked, such as chili and curries. With a little effort, a vegetable peeler will take off the skin, making it easier to slice the raw flesh and then cut it into cubes.

Kabocha, followed closely by acorn, turban, and butternut squashes, is the best stand-in for pumpkin. Kabocha is a Japanese variety and a relative newcomer to

JAPANESE-STYLE SQUASH

Kabocha is ideal for this because you can eat the skin. If you don't have kabocha, use peeled and cubed butternut squash or use delicata squash with the skin on and reduce the cooking time.

1 pound kabocha squash

2 tablespoons sesame oil

2 cups dashi or 2 tablespoons
   miso plus two cups water

1 tablespoon sugar

1 tablespoon rice vinegar

2 tablespoons soy sauce

Remove seeds and cut squash into 1" cubes. Heat sesame oil in a wide pan over medium-high heat. Add kabocha and cook until brown on each side. Stir together remaining ingredients and add to the pan. Cook, covered and without stirring, until the squash is tender but not falling apart, about 20 minutes.

our farmers markets. It is a deep green and round, but not spherical, and among the sweetest, richest types of squash. It is especially tasty sliced into wedges and roasted that way.

Spaghetti squash is a strange thing, indeed. Lemon yellow and the size and shape of a football, it stands out among its lumpy orange and green cousins. After baking it as described earlier, you can scoop out the flesh with a fork and watch it fall to stringy shreds. Toss these with butter and herbs or even your favorite spaghetti sauce. Because it's so stringy and watery, spaghetti squash is not particularly good for pureeing.

Thin-skinned varieties such as delicata should be kept in the fridge. Others will keep on the counter in a reasonably cool kitchen for a month or so. Keep in a cool place that doesn't freeze (basements and garages are often good for this) for longer storage.

When you're shopping for winter squash, don't overlook the homely, lumpy ones. But do look for ones that have no soft spots, are heavy for their size, and don't sound hollow when thumped.

1. Delicata squash. 2. Kabocha squash. 3. Pie pumpkins and winter squash.

GLUTEN-FREE SQUASH PANCAKES

By David Van Eeckhout

David Van Eeckhout, who farms at Hog's Back Farm in western Wisconsin, makes these pancakes for his family nearly every weekend. "I make a double batch so that we have extra to freeze for Monday or Tuesday's breakfast for the kids," he says. "They heat back up in the toaster great." Van Eeckhout recommends Pamela's Biscuit and Scone Mix for this recipe.

1½ cups gluten-free
    biscuit and
    baking mix
¼ cup cornmeal
¼ cup flaxseed meal
½ teaspoon salt
2 tablespoons butter
⅓ cup pureed squash
    or pumpkin
2 eggs
2 cups milk

Mix the dry ingredients together with a whisk.

Melt the butter in a small saucepan. Remove from the heat and add the squash and whisk until combined. Add the eggs and whisk until well combined. Slowly pour in the milk while stirring.

Pour the wet ingredients into the dry ingredients and whisk gently just until combined. Let the batter sit 10 minutes while your pan warms up.

Pour ⅓ cup batter onto a hot, oiled griddle or cast-iron pan. Flip when bubbles form on the surface. When using a gluten-free mix, use a large enough spatula to support the pancake well since they won't hold together as well as a pancake with gluten.

Makes 10 5-inch pancakes.

SWEET POTATOES

ALTHOUGH WE SOMETIMES call sweet potatoes "yams," you'll never see locally grown yams in a Minnesota farmers market. Yams are native to Africa and don't grow here. Sweet potatoes, while natives of South America, do have a handful of cultivars that will grow well in our climate.

Almost anything you can do with a white potato you can do with a sweet potato—with the caveat that sweet potatoes have more sugar and fiber and less starch than white potatoes, and that will affect the texture of your dishes. There is, of course, more than one kind of sweet potato to be found in the market and they will vary in flavor and texture. Generally speaking, the lighter the color, the starchier the sweet potato. The darker, more orange it is, the sweeter it will be.

Many people play up the root vegetable's natural sweetness by adding more sweetness—think of the traditional Thanksgiving casserole with marshmallows. But other cooks go the other way, countering the sweetness with heat and with the flavors developed when sugars brown. This browning reaction is one reason why sweet potatoes are so delicious roasted. It's almost impossible to make a crispy sweet potato oven fry without breading—and many, many kilowatts have been expended in this attempt—yet the lovely brown flavor is worth it nonetheless.

You can also roast sweet potatoes whole, and this is the easiest thing in the world: Poke a few holes in the skin and stick them in at 450-degree oven for about forty minutes. When a knife goes in easily, it's done. You can serve it as is, or scoop out the flesh and puree it with butter and seasoning (thyme and rosemary are nice) for a side dish. You've also got the beginnings of a soufflé or an unusual addition to pancakes or waffles.

At the market, look for sweet potatoes without any bruising or soft spots. Sweet potatoes don't sprout eyes as readily as white potatoes do, so you're

WHEN TO FIND IT

Sweet potatoes are usually harvested in October and November.

unlikely to see that. Look at the pointy tips of the potatoes: As they age, these will start to shrivel.

Store sweet potatoes in a paper bag somewhere dark and cool, but not in the fridge. Temperatures that are too cold change the texture. They will keep about a month. The peel is edible but tougher and not as pleasant as potato peels, so most people will remove and discard it.

★
The darker the sweet potato, the sweeter it will taste.

SWEET POTATO FRIES with SMOKY MAYO

By Karla Pankow

Karla Pankow farms with her partner, Elizabeth Millard, at Bossy Acres. Pankow jokes that the hard work and long hours of the growing season can mean farmers eat peanut butter sandwiches for dinner for three or four months out of the year; but in the slower months, she loves cooking up vegan treats like these.

2 large sweet potatoes, sliced into
   ¼" rounds, but with the peel still on
¼ cup olive oil
1 tablespoon cinnamon
2 teaspoons kosher salt
1 cup mayonnaise (can use vegan)
1 tablespoon lemon juice
1 tablespoon olive oil
¼ teaspoon cayenne pepper
   (or more, to taste)
1 teaspoon smoked paprika
Salt, to taste

Heat oven to 400°F.

Bring a large pot of water to a boil. Add sweet potatoes and cook 10 minutes. They will be soft, but not cooked through. Drain and pat dry.

Stir together oil, cinnamon, and salt in a large bowl. Add sweet potato slices and toss well.

Spread on two cookie sheets lined with parchment paper. Bake 20–30 minutes, until crisp, turning about halfway through.

Stir together remaining ingredients to make dipping sauce.

Serves four to six.

SWEET POTATO POMMES ANNA

Pommes Anna is traditionally made with white potatoes, which are starchier and bind together almost solidly in the oven. Sweet potatoes won't cook into a solid mass in your pommes Anna, but they will still look beautiful on the plate.

1–2 large sweet
   potatoes
¼ cup butter, melted
1 tablespoon mixed
   dried herbs (thyme,
   rosemary, oregano,
   whatever you like)
½ teaspoon salt

Heat oven to 400°F. Place a 9" cast iron frying pan in the oven to heat up.

Peel and slice sweet potatoes as thinly as possible. A mandoline is the best tool for this, but if you're working with a knife, aim for ¹⁄₁₀–⅛" thick. Stir together butter and herbs and toss with sweet potato, being careful to coat every slice.

Remove hot frying pan and carefully layer sweet potatoes in overlapping circles. Cover the bottom and sides of the pan, and then work your way up.

Bake about 30 minutes until a gently inserted knife meets resistance and when you lift the sides of the potato—again, gently—you can see a little browning.

Let rest about 10 minutes and then invert onto a serving plate.

TOMATOES

I F ANY VEGETABLE could be said to have a cult-like following, it is the tomato. Specifically, it is the fresh, truly vine-ripened tomato with the warmth of the summer sun still on its fat, ruby shoulders. A tomato that has ripened on the vine is almost a completely different vegetable from one that has been picked green and forced ripe with ethylene gas in a packing plant (as most grocery store tomatoes are). In the sun, it develops complex, meatier flavors and a more delicate texture.

Another difference is that commercial hybrids are bred for shipping—with a brutal toughness valued over flavor—but the open-pollinated cultivars (often called heirlooms) you are more likely to find in the market are bred for flavor. And many of them look almost nothing like the classic primary-red, spherical tomato. They've got lyrical names such as Green Zebra, Black Krim, Brandywine, Kumato—and appearances to match. They may be yellow, green, or purply black, pear shaped, flat-ish, or marked with deep caverns in their bulging sides. They may taste of citrus, plums, or rich, meaty steaks. A gracious seller will have a cutting board and some slices of unfamiliar tomatoes available to taste.

When you've had your fill of raw tomatoes eaten right out of hand (and this point will come, sooner or later in the season), they may start piling up on the counter. But there are countless ways to use and enjoy them. To paraphrase a certain bon vivant, when you are tired of tomatoes, you are tired of summer.

If you're still at the point in the tomato season when cooking your tomatoes seems like heresy—"I could make that with canned tomatoes in the winter!" you may be thinking—find ways to incorporate their raw, fresh flavor into other dishes. Grate a firm tomato—right there on the side of your box grater, nothing fancy—and use that in a vinaigrette, with, say an equal quantity of oil, a hit of vinegar, a pinch of sugar, and a little salt. Or, make

WHEN TO FIND IT

You'll know the **tomatoes** are in the market when the lines in the parking lot reach out to the interstate. That should, of course, be in August and early September.

✳

From classic round, red tomatoes, to heirlooms, to cherry tomatoes: They all taste better when they've been ripened on the vine, in the sun, and harvested that day.

a fresh tomato pesto, with two cups of fresh basil for every tomato, a little garlic, a little salt, oil to make a paste, and as much parmesan as you want.

Raw tomatoes are also the base of Spain's greatest gift to tomato-lovers: salmorejo. It couldn't be easier: Blend tomatoes (skin, seeds, and all), a little onion, a little bread, a little garlic, a *lot* of oil, and salt and pepper to taste until the mixture emulsifies and looks like creamy tomato soup—but tastes a world apart.

For many cooked dishes, such as sauces, stews, and fricassees, you'll want to peel your tomatoes. To do this, cut an X in the blossom end of each tomato and dunk it in boiling water for a minute, or until you see the skin at the X start to curl away. (Don't boil them too long; you just want to loosen the skin, not cook the flesh). Remove the tomatoes and let cool. The peel should come off easily with your fingers.

To seed tomatoes (whether you have peeled them first or not), cut them in half through the equator and either scoop out each section of seeds with a grapefruit spoon or give the tomato a gentle squeeze until most of the seeds and their gooey casings pop out. Seeding tomatoes can give you the texture you want for a salad or keep gritty seeds out of your sauce, but you end up removing a lot of flavor. Rather than discarding all that flavor, you can drink it: Seed the tomatoes over a strainer, scrape the liquid through to remove the seeds, stir a pinch of salt into the liquid, and you have pure essence of tomato in a glass.

Cooked tomatoes always appreciate a little sugar and a little acid to enhance their own tomatoey flavor but never enough to make the dish itself taste sweet or acidic.

Tomatoes, unexpectedly, love high heat: Fry wedges in a shimmering-hot pan to brown the sides for an English breakfast. Cut them in half and roast them; you'll have the base for a richly flavored tomato sauce, salad, or panzanella.

At the market, look for heavy, smooth tomatoes and give them a sniff—they should smell like tomatoes. You shouldn't see any wrinkling around the shoulders or any soft or bruised spots. If you are buying a half-bushel for canning or sauce, be sure to dig past the first layer.

At home, do not—repeat, do *not*—store tomatoes in the refrigerator. Temperatures that low change the flavor and texture of tomatoes almost entirely, making them bland and mealy. Instead, keep tomatoes on the counter in a single layer, not stacked on top of each other in a bowl. Some people will wrap tomatoes individually in newspaper and store them at about fifty degrees to make them last longer into the winter, but you have to have quite a few tomatoes to make this worth it, and their flavor will change.

Freezing tomatoes can be as easy as putting them in the freezer: whole, unpeeled. When you take them out, run them under warm water until the peel comes off in your hand, and then let them sit on the counter until thawed. They will be quite soft but perfect for soups and stews. If you want to be more formal about it, you can peel tomatoes as described earlier and freeze them in plastic bags with as much of the air sucked out of them as possible.

Drying tomatoes in the oven is worthwhile if you have quite a lot of them. Wash them extraordinarily well, slice them in half through the equator, and put them on a pan in the oven until they have shriveled. When they are crackly dry—no moisture left in them at all—you can let them cool and store them in an airtight container. Some people will store dried tomatoes in oil, but because of the risk of botulism, this is not recommended.

Use caution when canning tomatoes. Today's tomatoes are not as acidic as those of our grandparents' generation, which means that your old family recipe for tomato sauce may be too low in acid to safely can. A high pH, oxygen-free environment is exactly where dangerous botulism spores like to grow. Use a modern sauce recipe for canning and boost the acid in whole canned tomatoes with lemon juice.

Green tomatoes aren't common finds at the market, but there may be sellers clearing off their vines at the end of the season. Hard green tomatoes won't ripen on the counter and are too astringent to eat raw, but they are tasty—famously—fried. (Dredge in cornmeal and seasonings and cook each side on medium-low heat until brown.) They are also firm enough to pickle, either in a quick fridge pickle (just mix them with vinegar, water, sugar, and spices) or in your favorite cucumber pickling recipe. You can cook them down into chutneys (their flesh is firm, but will soften as you cook). And, deliciously, they can be baked into a sweet, apple-like pie.

GREEN TOMATO PIE

By Eric Larsen

Eric Larsen, who farms at Stone's Throw Urban Farm in the metro area, says he never even considered green tomatoes to be edible until his neighbors asked if they could have some of his. Now he loves to experiment with them and has even created a bread that uses the puree.

This green tomato pie, which could easily be mistaken for apple pie, came to him from a farmer he used to work with. The crust recipe, unusual because it is made with half butter and half oil, he learned from his dad.

Pie Crust with Oil

1½ cups all-purpose flour

1 teaspoon salt

¾ teaspoon baking powder

2 tablespoons flax meal

4½ cups tablespoons cold butter, cut into pieces

3 tablespoons canola oil

3½ tablespoons ice-cold water

Whisk together flour, salt, powder, and flax meal in a large bowl. Using a pastry cutter or fork, cut in butter until it is the size of rice. Drizzle in the oil, followed by the ice water. Using a wooden spoon and then your hands, mix until the liquids are fully incorporated and the dough holds together in a single mass. Knead the dough about 10 times to fully incorporate the oil. Taking two-thirds of the dough, roll out to a 10" circle, press into a greased 9" pie plate. Fill crust with desired filling. Roll out remaining third of dough to cover the top, seal at the edges by pinching with fingers, and bake according to your recipe.

Filling

4 cups thinly sliced green tomatoes

½ cup sugar

½ cup brown sugar

5 tablespoons flour

1 teaspoon nutmeg

¼ teaspoon cinnamon

1 tablespoon butter, cut into pieces

1 tablespoon white vinegar

1 teaspoon lemon zest

Preheat the oven to 400°F. Arrange a few slices of tomatoes on the bottom of unbaked pie crust to cover.
Mix the sugar through cinnamon in a bowl. Sprinkle 3–4 tablespoons over the bottom layer of tomatoes. Continue altering layers of tomatoes, sugar, and flour until the crust is full. Sprinkle any remaining sugar evenly over the top.
Dot the butter evenly over the top. Mix together the vinegar and lemon zest, and drizzle evenly over the top. Cover with the top crust, pinching the edges with your fingers to seal the crust. Cut a few slits to vent. Bake on top rack for 40 minutes. Serve warm topped with vanilla ice cream or at room temperature with freshly whipped cream.

GRAPE HARVESTER'S STEW

By Dara Moskowitz Grumdahl

For almost 20 years, Dara Moskowitz Grumdahl has covered food in the Twin Cities and Minnesota in nearly every imaginable form, from award-winning chefs to holes-in-the-wall to cheese makers, beer brewers, and farmers. Seriously, she's seen it all.

This is her take on the grape harvester's stew that Steven Brown once made at a short-lived restaurant called Rockstar. In place of sausages or chicken pieces, she says she'll use just about any local meat she has handy. You can even leave the meat out and make a hearty tomato stew for vegetarians. Grumdahl also notes that she loves the flavor of smoked paprika and will often use even more than called for here. Brown served his topped with a dollop of mayonnaise, and you could too.

2 tablespoons olive oil

4 fresh sausages or chicken pieces

1–2 tablespoons Pimentón
   de la Vera

1 cup minced onion

2 tablespoons minced garlic
   (3–6 cloves)

½ cup dry red wine

2 14.5-ounce cans
   fire-roasted tomatoes

4 thick slices of crusty bread
   (one per person)

Shaved Parmesan to serve

Pour olive oil into Dutch oven or other heavy pan. Heat over medium-high until shimmering. Place sausages in oil and cook until brown on each side but not cooked through. Remove sausages and set aside.

Add paprika and cook, stirring, about 1 minute. Add onion and cook, stirring, until just beginning to brown, about 5 minutes. Add garlic and cook, stirring, until fragrant, about 1 minute. Add wine and scrape browned bits from the bottom. Add tomatoes and bring to a simmer.

Return meat to the pan. Cover and simmer 15 minutes or until meat is cooked through.

Broil bread slices. Place one in each bowl. Pour stew over bread. Sprinkle with shaved Parmesan.

TROUT

WHEN YOU'VE HAD all the burgers and brats one summer can hold, your farmers market may have just the thing you need: local fish. The best part, if you're not an angler yourself, is that someone else has done all the work.

Most of the fish you will see at Minnesota farmers markets will be farmed rainbow or brown trout, usually frozen. There are also vendors who sell wild-caught salmon and halibut (delicious and, clearly, not local). Trout are related to salmon and have a similar flavor, but are milder and sweeter. Farmed rainbow trout get their red flesh from the food they're given, while in the wild their color might range from white to pink to red, depending on what they're eating.

Plan ahead to cook your trout: If you bought it frozen, you'll need to let it thaw in the fridge overnight. Don't try to speed up this process in warm water or—goodness no—in the microwave, as this will change the texture. Pat your thawed fish dry, rub it with just a little oil, and season it—a little salt and pepper is great, some dried herbs are even better.

The rule of thumb, no matter how you're cooking your fish, is ten minutes per inch of thickness. If you've stuffed a whole fish, remember to account for the extra thickness in the stuffing. You can grill fish over indirect heat (meaning you've got the grill hot and have pushed the coals over to one side or turned off one of the burners) or broil it on low.

To bake fish, heat the oven to 350 degrees F and heat an oven-proof pan over medium-heat on the stovetop. When the oil in the pan shimmers, place the fish flesh side down on the pan and leave it there to brown for about two minutes. Carefully flip it over and put the whole pan in the oven. Check it after five minutes.

Lenny Russo, who serves Minnesota trout often at his Saint Paul restaurant, Heartland, likes to cook it—among many other ways—entirely on the stovetop in a light crust of seasoned flour, wild rice flour, or cornmeal.

WHEN TO FIND IT
You should be able to find **smoked** or **frozen trout** throughout the season.

Always season your coating, he says, with a little salt, maybe some cayenne and herbs. If he uses cornmeal, he mixes up the fine and the coarse ground—the fine so it will stick to the fish and the coarse so you've got a little crunch. "I always cook the fish with the skin on," he says. "That's really important because there's a ton of flavor in the skin. The fat is between the flesh and the skin and from that fat is the flavor. And that's good fat."

Another way to bake fish is slowly, under a coating of some sort that keeps it from drying out. Baked fish covered in mayonnaise, like a "fur coat," is an old Russian trick. You can also blend roughly equal amounts of parsley and oil, with a little salt, into a paste and spread this over your trout fillet, covering it completely. Bake it in a 250-degree oven for thirty to forty-five minutes. It's almost impossible to overcook fish this way. Instead of flaking, it starts to almost melt.

Your vendor at the market may also have smoked fish. This is, to be sure, a flavor—and a smell—you either love or you hate. But those who love it really, really love it. When you get your hands on some smoked fish, flake off the flesh onto a salad. Or make an Old World sandwich on rye bread, spread with mustard or whipped cream cheese, maybe with some pickled beets or onions. Or blend it up with cream cheese or sour cream, lemon juice, and chives to make an irresistible dip or spread. Purists will leave out the dairy and pulse the fish in the food processor.

At the market, look for a vendor who has some samples to taste. That's the easiest way to know what you're getting. Also, spend a few minutes talking with the vendor. How and where does she catch or farm the fish? If they're farmed, how are they fed and what kinds of sustainability measures are in place? You may not know enough about fish farming to judge the answers, but you will start yourself on a path toward knowing where your food comes from.

Raw fish should be used or frozen within a day or two. Frozen fish will keep three months in the freezer or six months, or longer, in the deep freeze. Smoked fish will keep five to seven days in the fridge.

✳

Most of the fish at Minnesota farmers markets is trout, either rainbow or brown.

SMOKED TROUT GOUGERES

Julia Child taught America how to make and love gougeres—French cheese puffs—and this is her recipe, with a twist. It's hard to say whether Child would approve of the addition of smoked fish, but bacon and other cured meats are well-known additions, and smoked fish goes so well with cheese.

1 cup water

6 tablespoons butter

1 teaspoon salt

⅛ teaspoon black pepper

¾ cup flour

4 eggs

1 cup shredded sharp cheese, such as white cheddar

2–3 ounces smoked trout, skin removed, flaked gently with a fork

Preheat oven to 425°F.

Place water, butter, salt, and pepper in a heavy bottomed saucepan and bring to a boil. Stir until butter melts. Remove pan from heat and stir in flour. Place the pan back over medium-high heat and cook, stirring constantly and vigorously, until the mixture pulls away from the sides of the pan. This will happen quickly.

Now you need to keep working quickly. Pull the pan off the heat and make a well in the center of the batter. Break an egg into the well and beat it in immediately, followed by the remainder of the eggs, one at a time. Continue to beat about a minute, until the batter is smooth. While the batter is still warm, beat in the cheese and fish.

Use two spoons and make smooth 1" mounds on a baking sheet covered in parchment paper. Or scoop the paste into a large plastic bag, cut off a corner of the plastic bag, and squeeze it out like pastry cream.

Bake 20 minutes, until golden brown. As soon as you pull the gougeres out of the oven, pierce each one with a knife. This will allow the steam to escape and keep them from deflating.

GRILLED LAKE TROUT with BRAISED TURNIP GREENS and YOGURT SAUCE

By Lenny Russo

When Lenny Russo isn't cooking his fish on the stovetop, he likes to roll out the grill.

Trout

6 4- to 6-ounce lake trout filets

2 tablespoons grape seed oil

2 teaspoons sea salt

1 teaspoons white pepper, freshly ground

Sauce

12 ounces low-fat or whole-milk plain yogurt

½ cup green onions, coarsely chopped

2 tablespoons fresh dill, chopped

2 tablespoons grape seed oil

1 tablespoon lemon juice, freshly squeezed

1 teaspoon sea salt

½ teaspoon black pepper, freshly ground

Greens

6 cups turnip greens, stemmed

2 garlic cloves, minced

1 tablespoon whole unsalted butter

½ teaspoon sea salt

¼ teaspoon black pepper, freshly ground

½ teaspoon ground nutmeg

1 cup court-bouillon or stock

Rub the trout on both sides with grape seed oil, and season it with the salt and white pepper. Grill the trout on both sides until medium rare. Set the trout aside and keep warm. Heat the butter in a saucepan over medium low heat. Add the garlic. Sauté the garlic until tender, and add the turnip greens. Season with the salt, pepper, and nutmeg, and add the court-bouillon. Cover and braise until tender (about 2 minutes). In a nonreactive mixing bowl, combine the yogurt with the remaining ingredients and mix until well blended.

Evenly divide the greens between six serving plates. Place the trout on top of the greens. Top the fish with 2 ounces of sauce.

Serves six.

WILD RICE

WHAT DOES HOME taste like? For some Minnesotans, it tastes like wild rice. Our official state grain is nearly ubiquitous at potlucks in northern Minnesota—or, heck, really across the whole state—but is still an oddity in other parts of the country.

Wild rice, as any Minnesotan school child knows, is not rice at all, but an aquatic grass. It grows wild in deep waters that flow just a little but not too much. It's sensitive to all sorts of environmental pressures, from excess human activity to the changing of our waters. It is known as *manoomin* and held sacred by the Ojibwe people, some of whom still harvest it the traditional way, with a slow-moving canoe gliding through the water while the passenger bends the grass tops and knocks the ripe seeds into the boat. Most of the seeds actually end up in the water, however, ensuring strong regrowth in the years to come.

Some "wild" rice is now cultivated, and Minnesota leads the nation in its harvest. This called "paddy rice." Seeds of cultivated rice tend to be all the same size, shape, and color, while wild harvested rice is more irregular. Cultivated rice also tends to be darker in color. Minnesota regulates the timing and method of the harvest on state lands, and each Native American band has its own rules for harvesting and selling rice from its lands.

Wild rice tastes nutty and woodsy and, because its flavor can be quite strong, it is often mixed with long-grain brown rice in commercial "pilaf" mixes. Outside of Minnesota, of course.

Beloved Minnesota wild rice potluck dishes include hot dish, of course, and salads tossed with dried fruit, oil, and vinegar. And, who could forget, the beloved wild rice soup, whether creamy or brothy.

Before cooking wild rice, rinse it repeatedly in cool water until the water runs clear. You can then cook it either like rice (until it absorbs all the water) or like

WHEN TO FIND IT

Wild rice is harvested in September, but that means it is the time when you are least likely to find it at the market: The producers are busy harvesting. Otherwise, it is available throughout the season.

Wild rice adds a nutty, woodsy flavor to salads, soups, breads, and pancakes. You can also pop it like popcorn.

pasta (in excess water that you then drain off). Because how much water the rice will absorb and how long it will take to cook through vary so much (it is a wild product, after all), many people opt for the latter. If you prefer the former, use about four times as much water as rice and check it after twenty minutes (it may take up to forty-five). When it is tender, leave it on the heat a few more minutes uncovered, to cook off any excess water.

The simplest way to serve it is hot, tossed with olive oil or butter and salt. Woodsy wild rice also loves the woodsy flavor of wild mushrooms, so you could sauté a good handful of those and add them. You could cook it in milk instead of water and serve it with maple syrup for breakfast. Any leftover wild rice can be stirred right into your favorite cornbread batter or into a batch of pancakes.

And—who knew?—wild rice pops like popcorn. Heat a handful of kernels over medium or medium-high heat in a dry pan with the lid on. Shake the pan as you heat it; they will pop quickly.

Uncooked wild rice will keep just about forever in a dry place. Cooked wild rice will keep a week in the fridge and a month in the freezer, three months if you squeeze as much air out as you can and put it in the deep-freeze. Thaw the wild rice by giving it a quick dunk in boiling water and draining it.

WILD RICE WHEAT BREAD

By April Weinreich

April Weinreich, of Wahkon, Minnesota, has won many State Fair ribbons for her yeast breads. She often uses her bread machine to knead the dough, but this recipe also works if you prefer to knead it in a standing mixture or by hand. She notes that the water and buttermilk powder can be replaced with 1⅓ cup warm buttermilk or sour milk.

1⅓ cups warm water
2 teaspoons sea salt
2 tablespoons butter
¼ cup buttermilk powder
¼ cup honey
1 egg
2 cups bread flour
2 cups whole wheat flour
1 cup cooked wild rice
2½ teaspoons instant dry yeast

Combine all ingredients in a bread machine according to the manufacturer's instructions. Place on dough setting; if dough is too wet, add a couple of tablespoons of flour. If dough is too dry, add a couple of tablespoons of water. You can stop the machine and start over to knead the dough to your liking. After the dough cycle, form into two loaves and place in 8x4" loaf pans. Cover with a damp towel and let rise until double, about 1 hour.

Bake at 350 degrees for 28–30 minutes. Remove from pan and cool on rack.

CHICKEN WILD RICE SOUP

By Mary Helmerick

This soup, created by Mary Helmerick of the City of White Bear Lake Farmers Market, falls on the "creamy" side of the creamy versus brothy wild rice soup divide. "I have to make this for the whole extended Helmerick family every year for Christmas," she says. "If I don't, they are very disappointed!"

½ cup butter
¾ cup flour
¼ teaspoon salt
⅛ teaspoon pepper
¼ teaspoon poultry seasoning
1 tablespoon Worcestershire sauce
8 cups chicken broth, divided
2 cups cooked wild rice (preferably cooked
   in chicken broth)
1 pound fried bacon, cut into small pieces
2 chicken breasts, cooked and cut into small pieces
4 cups potatoes, boiled and chopped
2 pounds cheddar cheese, shredded
3 stalks celery, chopped
½ cup onions, chopped
4 cups half-and-half

In a large stockpot, melt the butter and stir in the flour, salt, pepper, poultry seasoning, and Worcestershire sauce. Cook, stirring constantly, until the paste thickens, about a minute. Stirring constantly, slowly pour in 4 cups of the chicken broth and bring it to a boil. Simmer until it has started to thicken. Turn the heat down to low.

Add remaining ingredients, except chicken broth. Add chicken broth gradually until the soup reaches the consistency you like.

ZUCCHINI and SUMMER SQUASH

POOR ZUCCHINI is the butt of so many jokes. When it's in season, it's the vegetable we can't get rid of fast enough, the one that takes over the garden and appears on neighbors' porches in a ding-dong-ditch effort to get rid of it.

But, really, zucchini is one of the hardest working vegetables we've got. It's available most of the summer, from tender baby zucchini in early July through the bonanza of August and well into September. Zucchini can be eaten raw, sliced into sticks or discs as a crudité or grated into salads. You can grate it and sauté it. You can slice it and grill it. You can toss it into the tail end of cooking a summer soup. You can stuff it and bake it. You can bake it into quick breads. You can pickle it. You can dehydrate it and make chips. You can stir it into a batter and fry it up in fritters. You can batter it and make tempura. And surely there are a thousand other uses desperate gardeners have thought up during the glut of zucchini season.

Really, we should be singing zucchini's praises for its versatility—and for its flavor as well. Zucchini is mild and summery and juicy, and it comes to life when pared with sharp flavors such as black pepper and balsamic vinegar.

Since zucchini is a variety of summer squash, everything you can do with a zucchini you can do with a summer squash (also known as yellow squash) as well.

Some summer squash look like yellow zucchini. Others have one bulbous end and a long, curving crookneck. You treat them essentially the same.

And another variety of summer squash that is growing in popularity and availability is the patty pan squash. These look like little flying saucers: bulbous discs with scalloped edges. They can be bright yellow, bluish green, or even off-white. They are often as small as two or three inches in diameter, but you might see them up to five or six inches across. And they are delicious. You eat the whole thing, skin and all. You can chop or slice them and sauté them, or you can show off their pretty shape by

WHEN TO FIND IT

Zucchini and **summer squash** come out in force in July and early August, but you may find some stragglers into September.

1. Pattypan squash. 2. Zucchini comes in a variety of shapes; the small ones are the most tender.

steaming them whole or roasting them sliced in half through the equator. They are also popular stuffed: Boil them until tender, slice off the stem end, scoop out the insides, mix that with cheese or rice or meat and lots of seasoning, and then bake them in a moderate oven for about twenty minutes.

There's no need to peel zucchini for cooking. When zucchini are young and small, smaller than an inch or an inch and a half in diameter, you can use the whole thing. With bigger zucchini, you'll want to cut out the pulpy mass around the seeds, which gets watery and slimy when cooked. The easiest way to do this is to quarter the zucchini lengthwise and then slice off the seeds on the diagonal.

You can also slice it in half lengthwise and then scoop the seeds out with a spoon or grapefruit spoon.

For flavor and texture, you really can't beat the baby zucchini, but as the season wears on, these will give way to mature vegetables. At the market, look for zucchini with firm, bruise-free skin that feel heavy when you pick them up. Look at the woody end where it was cut from the stem and see if it still looks relatively fresh. Pass over the ones the size of a baseball bat, which are likely to be woody, watery, and pulpy, not to mention unwieldy to cook with.

Don't wash zucchini until you're ready to use it. The moisture will speed rot. Keep it in a plastic bag in the fridge for a week or two. And, if you're drowning in it, it's time to start baking zucchini bread.

The fruit of the zucchini is not the only part of the plant we can eat. The young leaves are also edible (though you'll rarely see those in the market). You will likely see squash blossoms, however, in June and early July. These are delicate and delicious. These can be lightly battered (a light tempura-style batter is best) and deep-fried. You can stuff them with soft cheese and herbs before frying, or you can stuff them and bake them. They are delicious sautéed and then eaten on their own or added to tacos and quesadillas. To prepare the squash blossoms, pinch out the pistils from the middle of each flower and give it a gentle wipe with a cloth. They don't keep well at all, so plan to use them within a day or so of buying them.

BASIL ZUCCHINI SOUP

It only makes sense that zucchini and basil would get along as well as they do, bursting into profusion at the same time every summer. The drizzle of basil crema at the end is entirely optional, of course, but it makes this homey soup something you can proudly serve to friends. Crema is a thin, less-sour version of sour cream.

2 tablespoons butter

2 shallots

½ teaspoon salt, plus more to taste

1 cup fresh basil, packed, divided

3 pounds zucchini, chopped with the peel still on

6 cups mild, unsalted chicken or vegetable broth or water

1 cup Mexican crema, or sour cream thinned with a little water

In a large, heavy-bottomed pot, melt the butter and add the shallots and salt. Cook over medium heat until soft. Add half the basil, the zucchini, and the broth. Simmer, covered, about 30 minutes. Puree until very, very smooth in a standing blender.

Meanwhile, puree the cream or sour cream with the remaining half cup of basil. Drizzle over soup to serve.

Serves six.

ZUCCHINI AND FARRO SALAD

This filling salad brings together meaty, chewy farro and browned zucchini. Farro is also known as emmer wheat and can be found in the bulk aisle or near the pastas. Quinoa and bulgur wheat would also work well in this salad.

1 cup farro
1–1½ pounds zucchini, cut into ½" pieces
2 tablespoons olive oil, for cooking
Salt and freshly ground pepper to taste
¼ cup fresh mint, lightly chopped
1 cup crumbled feta
High-quality olive oil and vinegar, to taste

Bring a pot of salted water to a boil and cook farro 20 minutes, until al dente. Drain and set aside.

Heat 2 tablespoons olive oil in wide pan over medium-high heat. Add zucchini and sprinkle with salt and pepper. Cook until lightly browned, about 5 minutes. The zucchini should still be firm, not watery or too soft. Add mint, and cook for a minute more.

Stir together zucchini, farro, and feta. Taste and add salt if needed. Add a good glug of really good-tasting olive oil and vinegar to finish it.

Serves four.

RECIPES by CATEGORY

APPETIZERS

Smoked Trout Gougeres

Spring Pea Dip

BREAD

Wild Rice Wheat Bread

BREAKFAST

Blueberry Cornmeal Spoonbread

Gluten-Free Squash Pancakes

Scrambled Eggs Deluxe

CONDIMENTS

Daikon Radish Pickles

Honeycrisp Apple Mustard

Hot Pepper Vinegar

Kale Pesto

Marinated Cucumbers

Plum Catsup

Quick Red Onion Relish

Rhubarb Juice and Jelly

Spiced Honey

Sweet Corn Relish

DESSERT

Sour Cherry Chocolate Loaf Cake

Maple Caramel Sauce

Rhubarb-Blueberry Cobbler

DRINK

Watermelon Punch

MAIN DISHES

Bison in Papaya Marinade with Sauce Choron
Buffaloaf
Eggplant Parmesan
Eggplant Tomato Sauce
Fiddleheads and Bacon
Grape Harvester's Stew
Grass-fed Brisket
Green Tomato Pie
Grilled Lake Trout with Braised Turnip Greens
and Yogurt Sauce
Grilled Minnesota Pork Tenderloin with Heirloom
Tomato-Green Onion Relish
Grilled Mushroom and Roasted Garlic Pizza

Grilled Ribs with Plum Sauce
Lamb Kebabs
Piperade
Risi e Bisi
Savory Crepes with Smoked Salmon and
Blueberry Chutney
Savory Stuffed Apples
Slow-Roasted Garlic and
Winter Root Vegetable Gratin
Stuffed Onions
Sweet Vidalia Onion Pie
Warming Turkey Cassoulet
Yak and Green Chile Stew

SALADS

Baby Mixed Greens and Pear Salad
Fresh Shell Bean Salad
Herb Garden Salad

Pear Salad
Shaved Asparagus Salad
Zucchini and Farro Salad

SIDES

Albaloo Polow (Persian Cherry Rice)
Beet Risotto
Braised Escarole
Braised Kohlrabi
Cabbage and Fennel Slaw
Carrots Vichy
Cauliflower Tabouli
Charred Long Beans with Olives
Fancy Brussels Sprouts
Grilled Ramps
Japanese-Style Squash
Pan-Fried Garlic Scapes

Persian Cherry Rice (Albaloo Polow)
Potato Cauliflower Puree
with Agro Dolce Cipollinis
Roasted Beets with Lemon
Savory Stufffed Apples
Sesame Kale
Shaved Asparagus Salad
Simple Green Bean Salad
Spinach with Mushrooms
Sweet Potato Fries with Smoky Mayo
Sweet Potato Pommes Anna

SOUP

Basil Zucchini Soup
Chicken Wild Rice Soup
Chilled Asparagus Soup with Celery Seed Sour
Cream and Toasted Hazelnuts
Chilled Melon Soup
Couldn't Be Easier Broccoli Soup
Creamy Chicken Soup with
Baby Peas and Carrots
Cucumber Buttermilk Soup

Garlic Soup
Ginger-Carrot Bisque
Goat Phô
Knock-Your-Socks-Off Cauliflower Soup
Kohlrabi Coconut Soup
Pumpkin Soup
Smoky Split Pea Soup
Sweet Corn Soup
Zuppa Valdostana

PRODUCE by SEASON

ALL YEAR

Beef	Dried beans	Honey	Trout
Bison	Eggs	Lamb	Turkey
Chicken	Garlic	Maple syrup	Wild rice
Cornmeal	Goat	Pork	Yak

APRIL

Garlic scapes
Mushrooms

MAY

Asparagus	Garlic scapes	Mushrooms	Ramps
Beets	Herbs	Mustard greens	Rhubarb
Fiddleheads	Lettuce and tender greens	Onions (fresh)	Sunchokes
		Radishes	

JUNE

Asparagus	Currants	Mushrooms	Radishes
Bok choy	Fiddleheads	Mustard greens	Ramps
Broccoli	Gooseberries	Onions (fresh)	Raspberries
Chard	Herbs	Peas	Rhubarb
Cherries, sour	Lettuce and tender greens	Peppers	Strawberries
		Potatoes (new)	

JULY

Beets	Carrots	Gooseberries	Lettuce and	Peppers
Blackberries	Chard	Green beans	tender greens	Potatoes (new)
Blueberries	Collards	Herbs	Mushrooms	Radishes
Bok choy	Cucumbers	Kale	Mustard greens	Raspberries
Broccoli	Currants	Kohlrabi	Onions (dried)	Summer squash
Cabbage	Fennel	Leeks	Peas	Zucchini

AUGUST

Apples	Chard	Herbs	Mushrooms	Radishes
Beets	Collards	Kale	Mustard greens	Shell beans
Blueberries	Corn	Kohlrabi	Onions (dried)	Summer squash
Cabbage	Cucumbers	Leeks	Pears	Tomatoes
Carrots	Eggplant	Lettuce and	Peppers	Zucchini
	Fennel	tender greens	Plums	
	Green beans	Melons	Potatoes (cured)	

SEPTEMBER

Apples	Cauliflower	Fennel	Mushrooms	Rutabagas
Beets	Celery root	Herbs	Mustard greens	Shell beans
Broccoli	Chard	Kale	Onions (dried)	Sunchokes
Brussels sprouts	Collards	Leeks	Pears	Tomatoes
Cabbage	Corn	Lettuce and	Plums	Turnips
Carrots	Cucumbers	tender greens	Potatoes (cured)	Winter squash
	Eggplant	Melons	Radishes	

OCTOBER

Apples	Celery root	Mustard greens	Salsify (after the
Beets	Herbs	Onions (dried)	first frost)
Broccoli	Kale	Parsnips	Sunchokes
Brussels sprouts	Leeks	(after the first frost)	Sweet potatoes
Cabbage	Lettuce and	Potatoes (cured)	Turnips
Carrots	tender greens	Radishes	Winter squash
Cauliflower	Mushrooms	Rutabagas	

NOVEMBER

Beets	Celery root	Parsnips	Sweet potatoes
Brussels sprouts	Lettuce and	Potatoes (cured)	Turnips
Cabbage	tender greens	Rutabagas	Winter squash
Cauliflower	Mushrooms	Salsify	
	Onions (dried)	Sunchokes	

TECHNIQUES for COOKING VEGETABLES

BLANCHING

Few people will recommend boiling vegetables these days. You lose a lot of flavor and nutrients in the water, and you don't get a lot in the way of texture. Blanching, on the other hand, is a technique every cook should master. Blanching vegetables is a way to par-cook vegetables before freezing them or finishing their cooking in some other way. It's also a way to add a little panache to a summer platter of cold vegetables with dips and sauces. Done right, it yields veggies with bright color and a little bit of crunch.

Blanching is a two-step process. First, you need a big pot of water, well salted and at a rolling boil. For one pound of veggies, you want at least 1 gallon of water. The goal is to keep the water at a boil even after you add the vegetables or to bring it back to a boil quickly.

Then you need a big bowl of ice water. This is to stop the cooking immediately; otherwise, food will continue to cook, losing color and texture, as it cools.

Bring the water to a full, rolling boil; add a few tablespoons of table salt; and add the veggies, working in batches if you need to. Put the lid on to bring the water back up to a full boil as quickly as possible. Set a kitchen timer for 3 minutes for most vegetables, starting from when the water is boiling again. Carrots need 5 minutes.

Use tongs or a steamer basket to fish the veggies out of the boiling water, rather than dumping it into a colander. This way, you can bring it back up to a rolling boil and add another batch, either to avoid mixing vegetables or to avoid crowding the veggies. Submerge the vegetables immediately into the ice water. Drain and pat vegetables dry with a kitchen towel before serving or cooking further.

Toss whole blanched green beans, asparagus spears, baby carrots, or any other combination of veggies, with a simple vinaigrette and serve at room temperature on hot summer days.

FREEZING

Freezing is an easy way to keep ahead of the bounty of vegetables you keep bringing home from the farmers market and to preserve some of the best of summer's flavors for the cooler months.

Vegetables must be blanched before freezing. This preserves their flavor and texture. Otherwise, you'll defrost them and find a mushy, brownish mess. After removing vegetables from their cold-water bath, dry them thoroughly and pack them as tightly as possible into plastic bags, squeezing out as much air as you can. Vegetables frozen this way will keep one to three months in the freezer, longer in the deep freeze, and even longer if you have a vacuum sealer.

GRILLING

If you don't want to turn on the oven in the summer, you can develop a similar flavor on a hot grill. The key to grilling vegetables (or anything, really) is a clean, hot grill grate and an even coating of oil on the veggies themselves. Slice zucchini, eggplant, peppers, fennel, kohlrabi—or anything you like—into long, hearty strips. Toss them with the barest coating of oil, using your hands to coat every surface, season with salt, pepper, and herbs, and grill over high heat or hot coals until you get grill marks. A big platter of grilled vegetables is a showy centerpiece for an outdoor party.

You can buy a grill basket for grilling vegetables or fish. This keeps small or delicate pieces from falling through the grate.

PAN-ROASTING

A heavy-duty frying pan with a lid is another great tool for coaxing flavor out of vegetables. Cut veggies into bite-sized pieces and heat oil in the pan over medium-high heat until it shimmers. Add vegetables—green beans, broccoli, carrots, eggplant, sugar snap peas, or anything you like—and stir to coat in oil. Leave them there until they brown on one side. Next, stir them around, toss a little salt, pepper, and water (a few tablespoons) on them, put the lid on, and wait a minute or two. When they've softened up, remove the lid and cook until the liquid is gone. You'll get a toasty flavor and a great texture.

PICKLING

Pickling vegetables is a good way to stretch out their normal use-by date and to vary the flavors on your table. Just about any vegetable can be pickled. To make quick refrigerator pickles, slice vegetables—cucumbers, zucchini, carrots, beans, or anything you like—fairly thinly and pack them into clean jars. Discard anything even remotely close to rotting. Make a brine of vinegar, kosher salt (a teaspoon per cup of vinegar), sugar (to taste), and a mixture of whole (not ground) spices). Bring it to a boil and pour it over the vegetables. Store this in the refrigerator.

POACHING

Poaching preserves the fresh flavor of vegetables and a little bit of their crunch. You can also use a flavorful poaching liquid—call it a *court bouillon* if you're feeling French—to enhance the flavor.

Use a wide pan to poach. Pour in white wine, water, broth, or some mixture of them. Add fresh herbs and let it simmer a little bit. With the liquid truly simmering—that means it is below a full boil at 212°F and you should just see bubbles around the edges—add your vegetables and put the lid on. Leave long, skinny vegetables such as carrots, asparagus, and green beans whole and cut others into similar pieces. Hard vegetables will need about six minutes; soft ones, like zucchini, about three. Serve with aioli or a vinaigrette.

ROASTING

Roasting transforms the flavor of just about any vegetable. It may be hard to imagine turning the oven on to 400°F or 450°F on a hot summer day, but it can be worth it to taste the unexpected sweetness and nuttiness it brings out in carrots, asparagus, green beans, radishes, broccoli, cauliflower; even zucchini and cucumbers—really, anything.

Roasting describes a relatively high, dry heat. That means that if you cover your pan with aluminum foil, you're really baking or steaming the veggies in their own juices. Use as little oil as you can get away with, but use your hands to make sure the oil coats every surface of every vegetable. Sprinkle with a little coarse salt, but not much, as its flavor, too will intensify as the liquid comes out of the veggies and they shrink a little.

Spread veggies in a single layer and make sure they've got plenty of room—individual pieces should not touch each other—so that the liquid evaporates and you don't end up steaming the veggies. Cooking time will vary, but be bold and don't be tempted to take them out too soon. Give them time to develop a lovely brown color and a crust.

DIRECTORY of MINNESOTA FARMERS MARKETS

This directory contains listings for most of the farmers markets in the state. The handful of markets that aren't here are not registered with Minnesota Grown, the agency that keeps track of Minnesota farmers markets. Many thanks to Minnesota Grown for their help with this project and for the good work they do in encouraging and supporting local farmers and businesses.

Akeley Summer Market
Paul's Patio along the Heartland Trail, Akeley
Friday, 9 a.m.–1 p.m.

Albert Lea Farmers Market
www.albertleafarmersmarket.com
Broadway and Fountain streets, Albert Lea
Wednesday, 4–6 p.m.; Saturday, 9 a.m.–noon

Albertville Farmers Market
Central Park, Albertville
Thursday, 3–7 p.m.

Aldrich Arena Farmers Market
www.stpaulfarmersmarket.com
1850 White Bear Ave., Maplewood
Wednesday, 8 a.m.–noon

Alexandria Farmers Market
Broadway Street and Second Avenue, Alexandria
Tuesday, 9 a.m.–noon; Thursday, 3–6 p.m.; Saturday, 9 a.m.–noon

Andover Farmers Market
www.stpaulfarmersmarket.com
13655 Round Lake Blvd., Andover
Tuesday, 2–6 p.m.

Annandale Farmers Market
www.downtownannandale.org
City Hall Square, Annandale
Saturday, 8 a.m.–noon

Anoka Farmers Market
420 E. Main St., Anoka
Thursday, 2–5 p.m.

Apple Valley Farmers Market
www.stpaulfarmersmarket.com
7100 W. 147th St., Apple Valley
Saturday, 8 a.m.–1 p.m.

Atwood Memorial Center Community Farmers Market
720 S. Fourth Ave., St. Cloud
Monday, 10 a.m.–2 p.m.

Austin Farmers Market
Oakland Avenue and N.W. Fourth Street, Austin
Monday and Thursday, 3:30–6 p.m.; Saturday, 9:30–11:30 a.m.

Bagley Area Farmers Market
Highway 2 and Getchell Avenue, Bagley
Friday, 4–6 p.m.

Battle Lake Farmers Market
112 E. Main St., Battle Lake
Saturday, 9 a.m.–1 p.m.

Bayport Farmers Market
Perro Park, Bayport
Monday, 2:30–6:30 p.m.

Bemidji Area Farmers Market
www.bemidjifarmersmarket.com
200 S. Paul Bunyan Drive, Bemidji

Sunday, 11 a.m.–4 p.m.; Tuesday, 10 a.m.–
5 p.m.; Thursday, noon–6 p.m.;
Saturday, 9 a.m.–3 p.m.

Bemidji's Natural Choice Farmers Market
Second Street and Beltrami Avenue, Bemidji
Wednesday, 11 a.m.–6 p.m.;
Saturday, 8:30 a.m.–3 p.m.

Blaine Farmers Market
707 N. E. Eighty-Ninth Ave., Blaine
Saturday, 7 a.m.–noon

Bloomington Farmers Market
1800 W. Old Shakopee Rd., Bloomington
Saturday, 8 a.m.–1 p.m.

Braham Farmers Market
Freedom Park, Braham
Thursday, 3–7 p.m.

Lakes Area Growers Market
1001 Kingwood St., Brainerd
Tuesday, 8 a.m.–12:30 p.m.
Gander Mountain Parking Lot,
Highway 371, Baxter
Friday, 8 a.m.–12:30 p.m.

Brooklyn Park Farmers Market
8717 N. Zane Ave., Brooklyn Park
Wednesday, 3–7 p.m.

Buffalo Farmers Market
www.buffalofarmersmarket.com
100 N.E. First Ave., Buffalo
Saturday, 8 a.m.–noon

Buffalo Lake Farm and Flea Market
Buffalo Lake City Park, Buffalo Lake
Saturday, 8 a.m.–noon

Burnsville Farmers Market
www.stpaulfarmersmarket.com
3333 Cliff Rd., Burnsville
Thursday, noon–5 p.m.
200 W. Burnsville Pkwy., Burnsville
Saturday, 8 a.m.–1 p.m.

Camden Farmers Market
44th Street and N. Penn Avenue, Minneapolis
Thursday, 3–7 p.m.

Carlton County Farmers Market
1314 Minnesota 45, Scanlon
Saturday, 9 a.m.–noon

Centennial Lakes Farmers Market
7499 France Ave., Edina
Thursday, 3–7 p.m.

Central Minnesota Market
1480 N.E. Tenth Ave., Sauk Rapids
Saturday, 8 a.m.–1 p.m.

Champlin's Farmers Market
Ice Forum, Champlin
Wednesday, 9 a.m.–1 p.m.

Chanhassen Farmers Market
Seventy-Eighth Street and Market
Boulevard, Chanhassen
Saturday, 9 a.m.–1 p.m.

Chisago City Farmers Market
chisagocityfarmersmarket-org.webs.com
10625 Railroad Ave., Chisago City
Friday, 2–6:30 p.m.

City of White Bear Lake Farmers Market
Washington Avenue and Third Street,
White Bear Lake
Friday, 8 a.m.–noon

Cold Spring Farmers Market
First Street and S. Seventh Avenue,
Cold Spring
Wednesday, 3–6:30 p.m.

Columbia Heights Farmers Market
Fortieth and Jackson streets,
Columbia Heights
Thursday, 2–6 p.m.

Cook Area Farmers Market
127 S. River St., Cook
Saturday, 8 a.m.–noon

Coon Rapids Farmers Market
1555 N.W. 118th Lane, Coon Rapids
Wednesday, 3–6 p.m.

Crookston Farmers Market Association
Ash Street, Crookston
Tuesday and Friday, 4–7 p.m.

Dassel Farmers Market
Bandstand Park, Dassel
Friday, 3–6 p.m.

Delano Farmers Market
Highway 12 and County Line Road, Delano
Wednesday, 2–6 p.m.

Duluth Farmers Market
www.duluthfarmersmarket.com
E. Fourteenth Avenue and Third Street, Duluth
Wednesday and Saturday, 7 a.m.–noon

Eagan Market Fest
    1501 Central Parkway, Eagan
    Wednesday, 4–8 p.m.

Elk River Farmers Market
    716 Main St., Elk River
    Tuesday, 2–6 p.m.

Ely Farmers Market
    Whiteside Park
    Tuesday, 5–7 p.m.
    303 E. Sheridan St.
    Saturday, 10 a.m.–2 p.m.

Excelsior Farmers Market
    Water and Second streets, Excelsior
    Thursday, 2–6 p.m.

Fairfax Farmers Market
    S.E. First Street and Highway 19, Fairfax
    Tuesday, 4–6 p.m.

Farmington Farmers Market
    430 Third St., Farmington
    Thursday, 2:30–6:30 p.m.

Fergus Falls Area Farmers Market
    1110 W. Lincoln Ave., Fergus Falls
    Saturday, 9 a.m.–1 p.m.

Forest Lake Farmers Market
    Broadway and Lake streets, Forest Lake
    Tuesday, 5–8 p.m.

Fosston Farmers Market
    Melland Park, Fosston
    Saturday, 8 a.m.–noon

Fresh Start Farmers Market
    100 Main St., Baudette
    Saturday, 9 a.m.–2 p.m.

Fulton Farmers Market
    www.fultonfarmersmarket.org
    4901 S. Chowen Ave., Minneapolis
    Saturday, 8:30 a.m.–1 p.m.

Gaylord Farmers Market
    Fifth and Main streets, Gaylord
    Wednesday, 3 p.m.

Grand Rapids Farmers Market
    www.grfarmersmarket.org
    Highway 2 and N.W. First Avenue,
    Grand Rapids
    Wednesday and Saturday, 8 a.m.–1 p.m.

Harris Farmers Market
    www.harrisfarmersmarket.com
    Railroad Park, Harris
    Sunday, 11 a.m.–3 p.m.

Hastings Farm Market
    Highway 55 and S. Pleasant Avenue, Hastings
    Tuesday and Saturday, 8 a.m.–1 p.m.

Hector Farmers Market
    Highway 212 and County Road 4, Hector
    Wednesday, 3–6 p.m.

Hibbing Farmers Market
    www.hibbingfarmersmarket.com
    4114 W. Ninth Ave., Hibbing
    Tuesday and Friday, 8 a.m.–1p.m.
    City Hall, E. Fourth Avenue, Hibbing
    Thursday, 3–6 p.m.

Hopkins Farmers Market
    16 S. Ninth Ave., Hopkins
    Saturday, 7:30 a.m.–noon

Hutchinson Farmers Market
    8 S. E. Adams St., Hutchinson
    Wednesday, 2:30–5:30 p.m.; Saturday,
    8 a.m.–noon

Inver Grove Heights Farmers Market
    www.stpaulfarmersmarket.com
    8055 Barbara Ave., Inver Grove Heights
    Thursday, 3:30–6:30 p.m.

Kingfield Farmers Market
    www.kingfieldfarmersmarket.org
    4310 Nicollet Ave., Minneapolis
    Sunday, 8:30 a.m.–1 p.m.

La Crescent Farmers Market
    www.lacrescentfarmersmarket.com
    420 S. Second St., La Crescent
    Tuesday, 4–7 p.m.

Lakes Area Farmers Market Cooperative
    People's Park, Detroit Lakes
    Tuesday and Saturday, 10 a.m.–2 p.m.

Lakeville Farmers Market
    www.stpaulfarmersmarket.com
    210th and Holyoke, Lakeville
    Saturday, 9 a.m.–1 p.m.
    208th Street and Holyoke Avenue, Lakeville
    Wednesday, noon–5 p.m.

Lanesboro Farmers Market
    Sylvan Park, Lanesboro
    Saturday, 9 a.m.–noon

Lexington Farmers Market
    4175 Lovell Rd., Lexington
    Wednesday, 3–7 p.m.

Linden Hills Farmers Market
2813 W. 43rd St., Minneapolis
Sundays 9 a.m.–1 p.m.

Lindstrom Farmers Market
St. Bridget of Sweden Catholic Church
parking lot, Lindstrom
Wednesday, 3–6 p.m.;
Saturday, 8 a.m.–noon

Little Canada Farmers Market
61 Little Canada Rd., Little Canada
Monday, 9 a.m.–1 p.m.

Little Falls Farmers Market
S. E. Second Street and Highway 27,
Little Falls
Wednesday and Saturday, 7–11 a.m.

Malmborgs Inc.
2456 N.E. 125th Ave., Blaine
Wednesday, 3–7 p.m.

Mankato Farmers Market
www.mankatofarmersmarket.com
1400 Madison Ave., Mankato
Tuesday and Thursday, 3:30–6:30 p.m.;
Saturday, 8 a.m.–noon

Maple Grove Farmers Market
12951 Weaver Lake Rd., Maple Grove
Thursday, 3–7 p.m.

Maple Plain Farmers Market
Highway 12 and County Road 19, Maple Plain
Thursday, 3–7 p.m.

Market In the Valley
www.marketinthevalley.org
7800 Golden Valley Rd., Golden Valley
Sunday, 9 a.m.–1 p.m.

Market Monday (Sartell)
www.marketmonday.org
125 N. Pine Cone Rd., Sartell
Monday, 3–6 p.m.

Mentor Farmers Market
City Park, Mentor
Saturday, 8 a.m.–noon

Midtown Farmers Market
www.midtownfarmersmarket.org
2225 E. Lake St., Minneapolis
Saturday, 8 a.m.–1 p.m.; Tuesday, 3–7 p.m.

Mill City Farmers Market
www.millcityfarmersmarket.org
704 S. Second St., Minneapolis
Saturday, 8 a.m.–1 p.m.

Winter Markets Nov–Apr,
second Saturdays 10 a.m.–1 p.m.
(inside Mill City Museum)

Minneapolis Farmers Market
www.mplsfarmersmarket.com
Nicollet Mall, Minneapolis
Thursday, 6 a.m.–6 p.m.
312 E. Lyndale Ave., Minneapolis
Daily, 6 a.m.–1 p.m.

Minnesota Zoo
www.stpaulfarmersmarket.com
13000 Zoo Blvd., Apple Valley
Wednesday, noon–4 p.m.

Montevideo Farmers Market
Smith Park, Montevideo
Thursday, 3:30–6:30 p.m.;
Saturday, 8 a.m.–1 p.m.

Monticello Farmers Market
Monticello Library parking lot, Monticello
Thursday, 3:30–7 p.m.

Mora Area Farmers Market
Ole Park, Mora
Saturday, 8 a.m.–1 p.m.

Morris Area Farmers Market
www.morrisareafarmersmarket.com
E. Seventh Street and Colorado Avenue,
Morris
Mondays and Thursday, 3–6 p.m.

Morton Farmers Market
City Hall parking lot, Morton
Friday, 9 a.m.–3 p.m.

Mound Farmers Market and More
5515 Shoreline Dr., Mound
Saturday, 8:30 a.m.–12:30 p.m.

Nevis Farmers Market
Terrapin Station lawn, Nevis
Saturday, 9 a.m.–1 p.m.

New Hope Community Farmers Market
www.newhopemarket.org
4300 N. Xylon Ave., New Hope
Saturday, 8 a.m.–1 p.m.

New Prague Farmers Market
Baptist Church parking lot, New Prague
Wednesday, 3–6 p.m.; Saturday, 9 a.m.–noon

Nisswa Farmers Market
American Legion parking lot, Nisswa
Thursday, 8 a.m.–12:30 p.m.

North Branch Farmers Market
Eighth and Main streets, North Branch
Saturday, 8 a.m.–noon

Northeast Minneapolis Farmers Market
www.northeastmarket.org
Seventh Street and N.E. University Avenue,
Minneapolis
Saturday, 9 a.m.–1 p.m.

Nowthen Farmers Market
Between 199th Street and park entrance,
Nowthen
Thursday, 3–7 p.m.

Oakdale Farmers Market
1584 Hadley Ave., Oakdale
Wednesday, 3–7 p.m.

Olivia Farmers Market
Highways 212 and 71, Olivia
Thursday, 2–6 p.m.

Onamia Area Farmers Market
Highways 169 and 27, Onamia
Friday, 2–6 p.m.

Park Rapids Farmers Market
W. Fourth Street and Main Avenue,
Park Rapids
Wednesday and Saturday, 9 a.m.–1 p.m.

Paynesville Farmers Market
770 W. Hwy. 23, Paynesville
Saturday, 8 a.m.–noon

Pine City Farmers Market in the Park
Downtown Robinson Park, Pine City
Friday, 11 a.m.–1 p.m.

Pine River Market Square
Barclay Avenue and Third Street, Pine River
prmarketsquare.wordpress.com
Friday, 2:30–5:30 p.m.

Plainview Farmers Market
215 S.W. First St., Plainview
Wednesday, 4–8 p.m.

Plymouth Farmers Market
3650 Plymouth Blvd., Plymouth
Wednesday, 2:30–6:30 p.m.

Pope County Farmers Market
Pope County Fairgrounds, Glenwood
Tuesday, 3–6 p.m.; Saturday, 8 a.m.–11 a.m.

Princeton Farmers Market
www.pzfarmersmarket.org
Princeton Mall parking lot, Princeton
Saturday, 8:30 a.m.–noon

Prior Lake Farmers Market
www.priorlakefarmersmarket.com
Main Street just off Highway 13 and
County Road 21, Prior Lake
Saturday, 8 a.m.–noon

Ramsey Farmers Market
14544 E. Ramsey Parkway, Ramsey
Thursday, 3–7 p.m.

Red Wing Farmers Market
www.redwingfarmersmarket.org
212–290 Levee St., Red Wing
Saturday, 8 a.m.–2 p.m.

Redwood Falls Farmers Market
Second and Washington streets,
Redwood Falls
Tuesday, 2–5:30 p.m.

Richfield Farmers Market
636 E. 66th St., Richfield
Wednesday, 2–7 p.m.; Saturday, 7 a.m.–noon

Riverwalk Market Fair
Bridge Square, Northfield
Saturday, 9 a.m.–1 p.m.

Rochester Downtown Farmers Market
www.rochesterdowntownfarmersmarket.org
S.E. Fourth Street, Rochester
Saturday, 7:30 a.m.–noon

Rogers Farmers Market
21080 N. 141st Ave., Rogers
Wednesday, 3:30–7 p.m.

Rosemount Farmers Market
www.stpaulfarmersmarket.com
13885 S. Robert Trail, Rosemount
Tuesday, 1–5 p.m.

Roseville Farmers Market
www.stpaulfarmersmarket.com
2131 N. Fairview Ave., Roseville
Tuesday, 8 a.m.–noon

Saint Paul Downtown Farmers Market
www.stpaulfarmersmarket.com
290 E. Fifth St., St. Paul
Saturday, 6 a.m.–1 p.m.;
Sunday, 8 a.m.–1 p.m.

Sauk Rapids Farmers Market
www.saukrapidsfarmersmarket.org
VFW on Benton Drive, Sauk Rapids
Thursday, 3–6 p.m.

Savage Farmers Market
    www.stpaulfarmersmarket.com
    4800 W. 123rd St., Savage
    Sunday, 8 a.m.–1 p.m.

Scandia Farmers Market
    Gammelgarden, 20880 Olinda Trail, Scandia
    Wednesday, 4–7 p.m.

Seventh Place Mall Farmers Market
    Seventh Place Mall, St. Paul
    Thursday, 10 a.m.–1:30 p.m.

Shoreview Farmers Market
    4580 N. Victoria St., Shoreview
    Tuesday, 3–7 p.m.

Signal Hills Market
    Signal Hills Mall, West St. Paul
    www.stpaulfarmersmarket.com
    Friday, 8 a.m.–noon

South Saint Paul Farmers Market
    Seventh and Marie avenues, South Saint Paul
    Wednesday, 3:30–6 p.m.

St. Boni Market
    City Hall, St. Bonifacius
    Wednesday, 3–7 p.m.

St. Charles Farmers Market
    City Hall parking lot, St. Charles
    Thursday, 4–7 p.m.

St. Cloud Area Farmers Market
    www.stcloudfarmersmarket.com
    11000 W. Saint Germain St., St. Cloud
    Saturday, 8 a.m.–noon

St. Joseph Farmers Market
    www.stjosephfarmersmarket.com
    610 N. County Rd. 2, St. Joseph
    Friday, 3–6:30 p.m.

Saint Thomas More Farmers Market
    www.stpaulfarmersmarket.com
    1079 Summit Ave., St. Paul
    Friday, 1:15–5 p.m.

Staples Area Farmers Market
    Lakewood Health System parking lot, Staples
    Thursday, 3:30–6:30 p.m.

Stillwater Farmers Market
    S. Third and Pine streets, Stillwater
    Saturday, 7:30 a.m.–noon

Thief River Falls Farmers Market
    Pioneer Village, Thief River Falls
    Saturday, 9 a.m.–noon

Wabasha Farmers Market
    St. Elizabeth's Hospital, Wabasha
    Monday, 2–6 p.m.
    Heritage Park, under the bridge, Wabasha
    Thursday, 2–6 p.m.

Wadena Farmers Market
    801 N. Jefferson St., Wadena
    Friday, 2–5:45 p.m.

Warren Farmers Market
    Centennial Park, Warren
    Wednesday, 4–7 p.m.

Wells Farmers Market
    190 N.E. Third St., Wells
    Wednesday, 4–6 p.m.;
    Saturday, 9 a.m.–noon

West Broadway Farmers Market
    www.westbroadwaymarket.org
    900 W. Broadway Ave., Minneapolis
    Friday, 3–7 p.m.

Willmar Becker Market
    515 Becker Ave., Willmar
    Thursday, 3–6:30 p.m.

Winger Farmers Market
    18 N. Borud St., Winger
    Wednesday, 2–7 p.m.

Winona Farmers Market
    www.winonafarmersmarket.com
    N. Second and Main streets, Winona
    Saturday, 7:30 a.m.–noon
    Wednesday, 2–6 p.m.

Woodbury Saint Paul Farmers Market
    www.stpaulfarmersmarket.com
    2175 Radio Drive, Woodbury
    Sunday, 8 a.m.–1 p.m.

Worthington Farmers Market
    Second Avenue and Tenth Street, Worthington
    Tuesday, 4–7 p.m.
    Ace Hardware parking lot, Worthington
    Saturday, 6:30 a.m.–noon

Zimmerman Farmers Market
    www.pzfarmersmarket.org
    25850 Main St., Zimmerman
    Tuesday, 3–6:30 p.m.

CONTRIBUTORS

A special thanks to those who allowed us to photograph their stalls and produce, including Michelle Baar (preserves); Jim Pietruszewski (wild rice); Ames Farm (honey); Lee Family Farm (produce); Appleberry Farm (honey, herbs, wildflowers); Wang Ger Hang Farm (produce); Judy Vang (produce); B&D's Farm (produce); and many more.

Abby Andrusko
  Grassfed Cattle Company
  www.grassfedcattleco.com
  abby@grassfedcattleco.com
  612-581-7787

Claudine Arndt
  Minnesota Cooks
  www.minnesotacooks.org
  651-639-1223
  Wellness with Claudine
  www.wellnesswithclaudine.com
  claudine@wellnesswithclaudine.com
  612-202-7872

Carrie Boyd
  Onamia Farmers Market

David Brauer
  Fulton and Kingfield farmers markets

Steven Brown
  Tilia
  2726 West 43rd St., Minneapolis, MN 55410
  612-354-2806
  www.tiliampls.com

Faye Carroll
  Rivermist Farm

Atina Diffley
  organic consultant and author

Tammy Eichtens
  Eichten's Hidden Acres
  16440 Lake Blvd., Center City, MN 55012
  651-257-4752
  www.specialtycheese.com

Heather Hartman
  Mill City Farmers Market
  www.millcityfarmersmarket.org

Mary Helmerick
  City of White Bear Lake Farmers Market

Molly Herrmann
  Kitchen in the Market
  920 East Lake St. #107,
  Minneapolis, MN 55407
  612-568-5486
  www.kitcheninthemarket.com

John Hooper
  Hoopers' Christmas Tree Ranch
  15813 Christmas Tree Road
  Cold Spring, MN 56320
  320-685-4489
  yak-man@yak-man.com
  www.yak-man.com

Eric Larsen
  Stone's Throw Urban Farm
  2216 Elliot Avenue S.,
  Minneapolis, MN 55404
  612-454-0585
  www.stones-throw.herokuapp.com

Jeremy McAdams
  Cherry Tree House Mushrooms
  www.cherrytreehousemushrooms.com
  cherrytreehousemushrooms@gmail.com

Mill City Farmers Market
  704 S. 2nd St., Minneapolis, MN 55415
  www.millcityfarmersmarket.org
  Publishes *The Best*, weekly newsletter

Elizabeth Millard
  Bossy Acres
  bossy-acres@hotmail.com
  616-915-9027
  www.bossyacres.com

Dara Moskowitz Grumdahl
  food critic

Gregory Oja
  The Maatila

Karla Pankow
  Bossy Acres
  bossy-acres@hotmail.com
  616-915-9027
  www.bossyacres.com

Jane Peterson
  Ferndale Market
  31659 County 24 Blvd., Cannon Falls, MN
  55009
  507-263-4556
  www.ferndalemarketonline.com

Gail Rixen
  Bemidji's Natural Choice Farmers Market

Lenny Russo
  Heartland
  289 East 5th St., St. Paul, MN 55101
  651-699-3536
  www.heartlandrestaurant.com

Dorothy Stainbrook
  Heath Glen Organic Farm
  651-464-5290
  www.heathglen.com

Kristin Tombers
  Clancey's Meats and Fish
  4307 Upton Ave S., Minneapolis, MN 55410
  612-926-0222
  www.clanceysmeats.com

David Van Eeckhout
  Hog's Back Farm
  612-756-0690
  david@hogsbackfarm.com
  www.hogsbackfarm.com

April Weinreich
  Wahkon, MN

Carol Whitcomb
  J. Q. Fruit Farm & Orchard
  8082 33rd St., Princeton, MN 55371
  763-389-2567
  www.jqfruitfarm.com

Stewart Woodman
  Heidi's
  2903 Lyndale Ave S.
  Minneapolis, MN 55408
  www.heidismpls.com

Sue Zelickson
  food maven

Kathy Zeman
  Simple Harvest Farm
  9800 155th St. E., Nerstrand, MN 55053
  507-664-9446
  www.simpleharvestfarm.com

Andrew Zimmern
  chef, writer, and TV personality

INDEX

ABOUT THE AUTHOR

Her parents were her first and best teachers in the kitchen, but Tricia Cornell also learned to cook, in no small part, from the fresh produce and meats available in Minnesota. From farmers markets to a weekly CSA box to her tiny urban garden where she gathers herbs and fresh eggs, she finds daily inspiration to cook a little better and enjoy the experience a little more. Her first cookbook, *Eat More Vegetables* (Minnesota Historical Society Press, 2012), celebrated seasonal produce. The *Minnesota Farmers Market Cookbook* celebrates the growers, sellers, and chefs who do what they do so well with that produce. Tricia lives, writes, cooks, and eats in Minneapolis with her husband and two children.